24 Carat
BOLD

The Standard for
REAL Thought Leaders

Mindy Gibbins-Klein

24 Carat BOLD

The Standard for REAL Thought Leaders

Copyright © 2009 Mindy Gibbins-Klein

First published in 2009 by Ecademy Press
Second Edition published in 2011 by

Ecademy Press

48 St. Vincent Drive, St. Albans, Hertfordshire, UK. AL1 5SJ
info@ecademy-press.com
www.ecademy-press.com

Printed and Bound by Lightning Source in the UK and USA

Illustrations by Beatrice Buchser
Set by Philip Gibbins-Klein

Printed on acid-free paper from managed forests. This book is printed on demand, so no copies will be remaindered or pulped.

ISBN 978-1-907722-34-9

For Phil.   Thank you for being my rock.

For Tara and Bradley.
Always give your best and be willing to shine.

Acknowledgements

There are so many people I need to thank that I risk creating another entire book!

For extreme inspiration, helpful challenge and total encouragement and support I thank Andy Coote, Thomas Power, Penny Power, Dan Poynter, Mike Southon, Philip de Lisle, Brian Chernett, Mitch Herber, Judith Germain, Rob Brown, Penny Sansevieri, Carl French, Stuart Beattie, Jacqueline Beattie, Chris Roycroft-Davis, Molly Harvey, Graham Jones, John Donnelly, Bruce King, Peter Burton, Bob Ferguson, Alastair Dryburgh, Ron Rosenhead and Francis Nwofor.

For believing in me and helping me grow my business, I am eternally grateful to Sandi Klein, Tony Burgess, Julie French, Rhidian Jones, Louise Heasman, Ian MacMillan, Richard Norris, David Pinchard, Topher Morrison, Craig Goldblatt, Rory Murray, Marcus Cauchi, Sarah Watts, Philippa Hull, Andy Lopata, Alda Gant, Saroj Chumber, Emma Herbert, Bijay Shah, Frans Vogels, Clare Gillbanks, Don Hales, Sue Richardson, Cindy-Michelle Waterfield, Alan Stevens and Nigel Risner.

If I have forgotten to list you by name, please know that I do appreciate you!

Finally, I must thank every client I have ever worked with and every audience I have ever addressed, because it was seeing the light bulbs go on for you that helped me see the light. Thank you and keep on shining.

Contents

Introduction

My Light Bulb Moment

I keep meeting really talented people. People with something special to share and unique views and ideas. I'm sure it has something to do with my work as a book coach and leadership consultant, and it goes well beyond that. The individuals I encounter and coach have the potential to produce much more than just a book and to influence far more people than they ever imagined. It's just that despite their brilliant ideas, hard work and determination, many times they fail to achieve that elusive goal of being recognized as a top leader in their field, and I find that fascinating. I also find it fascinating that some people achieve the top spot with seemingly effortless ease. I began to think, 'there has to be a formula here somewhere'.

Since 2002, hundreds of people have come through my courses and private client programs, each with wonderful experiences, insights and wisdom to share, as well as inspirational goals for themselves and their work. Most have worked diligently to write and publish books and articles yet, over time, I realized that it is not about the books, articles or any other products they have produced. As with so many other worthwhile pursuits, I have found that the most important benefit was not the destination but rather the journey. It was the real progress these clients made in clarifying their thinking, putting structure to their ideas and establishing a realistic and effective strategy to share those ideas that truly made the difference. Yes, many great books were born and these books often sold many hundreds or thousands of copies, attracted media attention and won business for the authors. However, something else was created during the process, something even more extraordinary: thought leaders. People who lead and influence others with their thinking.

The first time I used the term 'thought leaders' in relation to my clients, I got a good response from the audience I was addressing. But then I started hearing it in different contexts and describing people that I did not necessarily agree were exceptional. I began to get annoyed at the apparently arbitrary use of the label and the lack of proof or quantifiable evidence. It also seemed that the lists were too esoteric, with very few people being recognized. I knew I was working with some amazing thought leaders who were building their reputations by sharing valuable ideas with a wide audience. So I decided it was time to put some parameters around this whole topic and give more – not fewer – people the guidance and direction they need, so they have a chance to shine.

I would like to say that I created the REAL thought leader concept in a flash of inspiration, like the proverbial light bulb going on. However, it was more of a gradual realization which grew stronger the more I spoke to people and shared the idea. My light bulb moment has taken about a year, so perhaps it is more like the new long-life bulbs that start out dim and get brighter and brighter. It is pretty clear to me now, although not perfect (if there is such a thing), but it seemed the right time to capture my thinking in a book. So many people wait and wait until they get their concept 'just so' and sadly the book never comes out.

Don't Like the term 'Thought Leader'? Then Focus on REAL

You will find as you go through the book that the focus is on a distinct set of attributes (REAL) which can be embraced by anyone, and you don't even have to use the phrase 'thought leader'. It is just a convenient term which is self-explanatory, and it is generally accepted in the business world. Most importantly, however, it encapsulates the way in which real change happens – and it always starts with someone bold enough to share his or her thoughts in a positive and constructive way to make things happen.

Take it Personally

I have intentionally written this book in a very personal style. I have used the word 'you' throughout the book and when I say 'you', I mean 'you', the individual. The perception of a company as a thought leader is usually false, as a company can only be a by-product of its executives and their thought leadership. That leadership creates the culture that then gets seen and judged by the outside world. The only way to shift the culture is to strip things back to the people at the helm (I guess that would be you?) and then build again from the core.

> A company can only be a by-product of its executives and their thought leadership.

The other reason I have written the book in this way is that I care about you as an individual and want you to succeed as a leader in your business and in your life. If I were there in person, you would get a full sense of the passion I have for this subject and the trust and confidence I have in you to make a significant contribution to the leadership of our business community and to society as a whole. Five percent of business owners are doing what it takes to play at the top of their game and, as a result, they are winning even in a tough business environment. Unfortunately, though, too many would-be leaders shy away from their right and their responsibility to effect lasting change because of their insecurities and fears. Over ten years of working with some of the greatest leaders in the world, I have seen how it is possible, with a leap of faith and some dedicated time and effort, to overcome seemingly insurmountable problems and boldly rise to the challenge of inspiring and leading others.

I wish more people would take that leap of faith. I hope that by the end of this book you will feel excited and empowered to do so. The rewards are significant: more business, higher fees, recognition, better client loyalty and a great sense of achievement and satisfaction.

Bold and Opinionated

Sometimes my views may come across as too strong or forceful. If you find yourself reacting to challenging statements, stop and remember that the intention with which I have written this book is one of pure caring and encouragement. One of the messages you will find in this book is that people need to be bold and opinionated, yet respectful, to get results. It is a fine and delicate balance which, unfortunately, very few leaders in business and in society on the whole, get absolutely right. I hope I have achieved that balance because that is what can create shifts in thinking, action and outcomes.

It starts with you. There are some provocative thoughts throughout the book which are meant to do just that: provoke thought. You may need time to digest the material, and that can continue long after your first read-through. There are also some exercises in the book, and I have included them with the full knowledge and understanding that most people, including myself on many occasions, skip through exercises of this nature, preferring to do them later, and in some cases not at all. I have told my clients for years that you can only put your best material in its best format into the market with the best intentions. After that, there is very little that you can control. So, knowing that, I urge you to get involved as you read this book. We don't always like writing in books; in fact, we were told as children not to write in our books. I'm telling you it's OK. But if you still don't want to, you can use separate pieces of paper. Or at least answer the questions in your head. However you end up engaging with the material, my fervent wish is that you take it and use it to take your thinking, and in turn, your life, to the next level.

Chapter 1
Why We Need Thought Leaders More Than Ever

What is this 'Thought Leadership' stuff anyway?

According to Wikipedia, 'thought leader is a buzzword or article of jargon used to describe a futurist or person who is recognized among their peers and mentors for innovative ideas and demonstrates the confidence to promote or share those ideas as actionable distilled insights.' I heard the term for the first time in about 2006 but it has been around since the mid-1990s. As I mentioned earlier, by 2008 I was becoming disillusioned with the way certain people were abusing it.

In the absence of any standards or criteria, many consultants come up with their own definitions, which are not always specific enough. For example, the *Financial Times* published an article on December 9th 2008 entitled 'What's the Big Idea?' In it, they explored the area of thought leadership and put forward the following definition created by a consultancy called TLG, assisted by Henley Business School:

'The ability to develop and communicate pioneering and rigorous ideas that are relevant to society and influence people's behaviour'.

This definition could be better and more precise, in my view.

The final straw was when I heard someone being described as one of the top thought leaders in the country and I didn't agree. Moreover, I knew of other worthy individuals whom I believed were adding more value and making a difference, but were not being recognized. Looking into the matter, I discovered that there are academic bodies making determinations and decisions about who is on the list! As a dyed-in-the-wool marketer, I believe that the market decides who the leaders are. The term 'thought leader' is probably here to stay, so I have made it my mission to provide context, criteria and strategies to ensure a level playing-field and maximize the impact of some very promising individuals.

Why is Thought Leadership Necessary?

Through my annoyance, I could still see the relevance in identifying and recognizing true thought leaders. Our planet and society are facing enormous, unprecedented challenges that only new thinking will resolve. In fact, the extreme nature of recent economic problems has brought this issue (or opportunity) to a head. It is more important than ever to embrace new thinking; therefore we need potential thought leaders to 'step up to the plate' and deliver their best ideas in the most effective and impactful ways. Now, that's exciting!

The Rules have Changed

If there is one lesson to be learned from the downturn of 2008, it is that we should expect the unexpected. Business levels can plummet faster than anyone would have predicted, clients can go out of business, weakening a supply chain as well as confidence levels; big companies are no more secure than smaller ones. The resultant trend of purse-string-tightening means less money on the table, fewer deals and more pressure on those still in the game to compete and win their share of that smaller pie.

Many companies have become more risk-averse and cautious about decision-making and expenses. This leads to more people choosing to work with the 'safe bet', the top leader, the proven solution. That top leader is usually a thought leader as well, showing agility and innovation and keeping ahead of the pack, especially in stressful times.

People are Busier than ever and Suffering from Information Overload

Apparently, the information available on the Internet is doubling every few months. Even if you tried to scan every web page currently online, it would take you about five hundred lifetimes. This is a sad commentary on the way our society is heading. It seems that quantity has won a significant battle over quality, and it is becoming harder and harder to find the needle in the ever-increasing haystack.

I get upset when I need to wade through lengthy newsletters completely lacking in value, unsolicited manuscripts that should have been written with more care or, worst of all, books that promise the earth and deliver very little. My time is too precious and I imagine yours is, too.

Most business leaders I know receive between one hundred and two hundred legitimate emails per day. Some people I speak to deal with as many as one thousand messages a day! They can hardly keep up and feel overwhelmed most of the time. I know that when I feel the pressure of too many emails, I just delete everything that isn't essential. How am I supposed to assimilate all that extraneous information? At this point, something really needs to stand out to get my attention.

Even though more and more people are becoming self-employed, the number of hours they are working is rising sharply. There is always one more call to make, one more deal to close, one more email to send. In part it is because, as owners of the business, they are so committed to their work and can see the value of working hard to achieve more and reap all the rewards. But the scarier truth is that the 'overworked, constant, Blackberry permanently on' mode is now the accepted and expected way of working. We know there is something wrong with our culture but we don't know how to stop the carousel and get off – or at least slow it down.

And I think you'd agree that some people have become absolutely addicted to the internet and feel they have to read everything that comes across the screen (which we have just said is impossible). The result of all this is an unprecedented level of stress which we think is due to situations and circumstances out of our control. Where are you on the stress scale these days? Even my own teenage children are getting caught up in this, especially my daughter who spends every free moment checking her Facebook messages and conversing in real-time with her friends on MSN. We had a 'no-screen day' a few months back because the situation was becoming intolerable, and it was amusing to see her start to head for the keyboard several times and then remember she wasn't allowed to touch it. It's become a habit.

Channel-hopping Culture

The barrage of information can cause us to flit from one thing to another, to scan documents quickly instead of reading them thoroughly. We think that maybe we will be able to catch the main ideas, but we are asking our brains to apportion our concentration across too many things. I like to call this a 'channel-hopping society'. If we don't like what's on TV, we just click the button and we can watch any one of hundreds of other channels. Program not captivating enough? Click. Not exciting enough? Click. Too demanding? Too boring? Click. Click. Our youngsters have the attention span of a flea and we are not much better. I think where there is so much information competing for our attention, the only strategy is to scan it all quickly and see if we can make sense of it. But the danger in scanning things quickly is that you cannot truly get into the essence of the message in the same way as when you focus. Malcolm Gladwell, in his incisive and accurate book *Blink: The Power of Thinking without Thinking*, suggests that not only should we be unconcerned with the inability to process the large number of data being presented to us in any given moment, but we can rely on our instincts and intuition, especially when we have studied the subject and become experts. I'm not so sure I agree.

Lost People Need Direction

If there is one thing we can count on, it is the fact that we cannot count on anything. The only certainty is uncertainty. Having seen an economy nearly collapse in record time, currency, gold, property and the stock market in freefall, a large number of people are genuinely worried. Jobs are not secure, governments, it seems, cannot be trusted to follow the wishes of their constituents. The changes are more dramatic than ever, with the pace of change faster than ever.

There is also a worrying trend among our young people in terms of the people they are turning to as leaders. Are those leaders providing the right kind of direction, the kind that will encourage and support the next generation? A few years ago, we were driving in the countryside as a family and my daughter (eleven years old at the time) asked if we could play some of her music on the car CD player. I had just allowed her to buy a CD by a very prominent rap artist after she assured me that she would not be influenced by the lyrics. I had never heard the lyrics before but I had been told there was quite a bit of swearing. When the CD came on, I listened to words of rage and depression, and I was overcome by a terrible feeling of sadness for our society. The more I listened, the more upset I got until I finally took the CD out of the player, tears streaming down my face. I told Tara to get rid of the CD, but she had spent her own money on it. So I offered to pay her back the £10 and destroy the CD so no one else would have to listen to it; that's how upset I was.

What is going to happen to our youth if they follow the

wrong leaders? I dread to think of the worst possible scenarios. We don't need such extreme examples to acknowledge that the lack of right, principled thinking could leave the next generation without sufficient direction and guidance.

Looking for the Next Generation of Thought Leaders

So who will step forward and lead the way? We need a new batch of real thought leaders, people who can take our society into the next phase of its evolution and bring the kind of transformation that is so sorely needed. The obvious candidates come from business and government, not the media. The celebrity culture so popular today is flawed because it celebrates the wrong things. There is nothing wrong with people gaining popularity for entertaining us. I do have an issue, however, when they become popular simply because of their wealth, looks or peer group, and it engenders in others an aspiration to achieve higher levels of material wealth and lifestyle which, in turn, can cause enormous stress and feelings of inadequacy.

> We need a new batch of real thought leaders, people who can take our society into the next phase of its evolution and bring the kind of transformation that is so sorely needed.

With a few notable exceptions, celebrity does not offer enough substance to provide direction to people on important issues beside entertainment. The exceptions that leap to mind are Brad Pitt and Angelina Jolie using their celebrity status to create change in disadvantaged communities in the third world, and Arnold Schwarzenegger using his previous popularity to get into public office in California and progress society from a political platform.

Thought Leaders Get More Business and Higher Fees

In every segment of society – business, politics, science, social innovation or entertainment – there are people who rise to the top of their league and become known for their ideas. They stand out because they stand for something and they get the attention of the influencers in their area. This, in turn, creates the momentum for a tidal wave of change, spurred on by this new insight.

In business, there is a direct correlation between the position of leading expert in one's field and increased levels of business and income. As a member of the Professional Speaking Association in the UK, I network with many people who have achieved the elevated status of 'top person in their field' and when they have something new, original and of value to share with their market, people listen. They can also command fees that are significantly higher than their peers. I know because I often find myself in this category (this said most sincerely and humbly!). It has taken several years to spread the word widely enough to develop this reputation as a thought leader, and now I can look back and chart the journey retrospectively. I also see very clearly that my journey would not have led to this place if I had not had the right motivation.

Motivation to Be a Leader

How Big is Your Ego and Does It Matter?

What is 'ego'? Is it a good thing or is it a bad thing? So many people come to me for book projects saying "It's not an ego trip." As if I were going to judge them. Personally, I think it's great to have high self-esteem and want to be famous because that means we will strive to do important things.

As human beings, we need to feel important. This is a basic human need that starts early in childhood. According to the psychologists, when we start to doubt our parents' love and feel any kind of lack of attention, we do whatever it takes to get it back. Where ego becomes a problem is when it is the primary driver of one's actions, or when it leads to putting someone else down in an effort to make oneself seem superior. Any psychologist can explain how these extreme cases of attention-seeking and significance-driven behavior occur because of a feeling of lack or inferiority, possibly even pathological reasons stemming from childhood experiences. In general, though, we all have a healthy need to feel important.

Ask yourself right now: "On a scale of 1 to 10, how important do I want to feel to those closest to me? In my family? At work?"

If your answer was a 9 or a 10, this is not only a need but it will be a driving force in your life. You will make decisions and act based on fulfilling that desire to feel important. Let me be clear: there is nothing wrong with that! In fact, I worry more about people who don't take care of their own needs, whether it's because they feel like playing the martyr or they truly don't value themselves enough.

I have been living in the United Kingdom for nineteen years and I have heard hundreds of people tell me that it is not British to blow one's own trumpet or rise above one's station (yes, this term is still in common use and so is 'too big for his britches'!). In fact, I have heard people make derogatory comments about colleagues or neighbors who talk too proudly of their accomplishments. Drawing unnecessary attention to ourselves is frowned upon in our society.

There is a fine line between being proud and showing off, though, and it all depends on the context. I happen to believe that if you are in business, you need to find a way to promote yourself or you will not succeed. This is basic marketing. If you don't like blowing your own trumpet, get someone else to do it for you. Outsource your marketing and promotion and get your network to boost your profile. Be aware, however, that whatever methods you choose, you will still need to lead the program and guide the agency or your advocates so you end up with the results you want.

My Study – 50% Want Recognition

In January 2008, I conducted a study among several hundred clients. I asked them what their top reasons were for wanting to write and publish a book. Over half said they would do it for recognition or fame. As I said, there is nothing wrong with that! In some cases, this desire comes from a situation of lack or scarcity. We find ourselves in situations where we question our importance and our value to others and to society. We are made to feel less than adequate and less than others in this celebrity-driven culture. How many times have you looked in a newspaper or magazine and felt annoyed about someone less talented than you, less hard-working or simply less interesting, getting all the publicity? Be honest! What about when other people seem to be attracting all the attention and getting all the credit, or even all the business? Doesn't feel too good, does it?

What are the alternatives? I see only two: sit in the corner and moan bitterly about it to your friends and anyone else who will listen, or develop a strategy to become the one who attracts all the publicity, interest and business.

Leave a Legacy

We also have an innate need to leave a legacy for the next generation. Nobody likes to think that they didn't produce anything important during their lifetime, that their life didn't matter.

Ask yourself how you would feel if you knew you were going to die tomorrow. Do you feel that there is something of yours that would remain here, by which people would remember you? How strong is your desire to leave a legacy of some kind?

> Nobody likes to think that they didn't produce anything important during their lifetime, that their life didn't matter.

Most of us want to make our mark on the world, something that will go on even after our career has ended, and maybe even after we are no longer around. My own father spent many years wishing that he had followed his dream of writing screenplays. When he retired at the age of 65, he immediately got back in touch with his dream and spent the next twenty years writing. During that time, he produced five full-length, well-researched screenplays as well as some musical presentations which he produced and directed in his town. We were very proud of him, and he received much recognition on a local basis. However the one elusive goal he pursued relentlessly was that of a major studio producing his screenplays, or even seeing them on television. My dad had some great stories and messages to share with the world and he wanted them to be shared as widely as possible. What he may not have realized in his lifetime was that he was already wildly successful simply having written those plays. His legacy lives on whether the screenplays are made into films or not.

Influence

Finally, I have noticed that the majority of people in leadership roles not only like to influence others but they are good at it. Influence is an essential skill of a good leader, yet people don't always know how to exert their influence in the right way, or they shy away from the best opportunities. Back to that British reserve, it can stop good people from getting an important message into the market.

If you want to be a REAL thought leader, you will need to influence people.

> With a position of power comes the
> responsibility of influence.

We have all seen reluctant leaders, thrust into positions where the demands to provide influence and strong leadership put them beyond their comfort zone. Sometimes these reluctant leaders astound those around them and rise to the challenge. When they fail, however, they are accused of shirking their responsibility and being weak. Be honest. Have you ever wished that you could just have 'an easy life' for a few days? I have felt that way several times in my life, most notably when I needed to downsize and finally outsource a department I had built up from the ground. I had twenty-five loyal and dedicated employees to think about, one newly married, two about to get married, one pregnant and one around retirement age with few chances to secure another job. I also needed to organize the seamless transfer of a multi-lingual, multi-national call center that thousands of people relied on to get through to the company.

> You cannot walk away from your sphere of influence; it is always there.

Between the pressure of senior management and the worries and concerns of my staff, I felt squeezed and frightened. More than once, I had fantasies about hiding, turning back time or even quitting, but then I remembered that leaders have to take the good with the bad, and people trust them to make good decisions. Anyway, you cannot really walk away from your sphere of influence; it is always there.

Competitive Marketplace

We live in a very competitive world and it is becoming more so every day. The speed with which information is flowing means that it is harder than ever to maintain a competitive edge for long. The internet has created a smaller world; it has also created a smaller window of opportunity to create new things and be unique before the imitators and competitors start snapping at your heels. Every time I deliver a talk on this subject, people come up to me at the end and ask me how they can be unique. I believe that is the wrong question. There is very little in our world that is truly unique and therefore people can waste a lot of time and energy pursuing that goal. More important questions involve how to gain market share, how to keep the clients you have and how to be the best that you can be.

You are already unique. Striving for it will only induce stress as you spend your time looking around instead of ahead. Picture yourself in a race. There are runners all around you and everyone is staring ahead intently. The gun goes off and everyone is flying around the track. You suddenly get a sense that your nearest competitors are very close to you. You glance around you, to the side and even try to glance behind as you keep running at your fastest pace. I guarantee that you will have slowed your pace while looking around and, depending on how far you turned your head, you may have even stumbled because you stopped looking ahead.

I'm not saying that you should put your head in the sand and ignore the competition in your field or pretend they don't exist. That would be stupid and bad business practice. What I am saying is that too many business leaders obsess with differentiation and suffer because of it.

You should always know what other companies in your industry are doing and a healthy sense of competition keeps you fresh and on your toes. I have created some of my best and most creative material in response to competitive threats. You want to know who your competitors are, keep up with their offerings and, most importantly, ensure that they are not attracting your clients. But an obsession with others and what they are doing causes many potential leaders to slip down the ladder instead of moving up. I have seen this so many times, especially with authors. They read others' books, they worry that theirs will not measure up. They spend so much time worrying about that instead of creating excellent new material that it becomes a self-fulfilling prophecy!

What is NOT Thought Leadership?

Celebrity

Unfortunately the thought leaders that leap to mind are not necessarily the ones that we want influencing our children, our employees or our friends. As I mentioned before, celebrity is valued too highly in our society. People look to celebrities as role models and use those references to determine their own goals and attitudes. In previous generations, celebrities provided entertainment but the celebrity world was inaccessible and untouchable. Now things are different, with many celebrities on reality television shows and social networks, writing books and giving interviews that give readers detailed information about their lives. The increased proximity and intimacy gives many people the illusion that they too can be a celebrity. As a result, for many people, celebrity culture has become the aspiration, instead of more realistic and worthwhile pursuits.

Size Does Not Determine Leadership

Think of some big name companies that were leaders in their industries only ten or fifteen years ago. Many are not only falling short of their previous glory, but they are actually falling behind other, more innovative companies. The previous leaders, in many cases, are becoming dinosaurs. Just because a company has been around forever or has millions of shareholders, that does not give it the right to call itself a leader. In fact, wouldn't you agree that the bigger the company, the more risk there is of major problems? We have seen the collapse of huge corporations over the past few years because of cash or profit challenges. I have worked at several large corporations and seen the problems they encountered in challenging times, such as large overheads of real estate and staff, trying to shift processes and procedures across multiple sites and tens of thousands of employees and generally trying to manage the organization with five to ten layers of management in place. It has been said that you cannot turn a tanker on a dime, and when times get tough it is much harder for the larger organizations to react swiftly.

Many companies do have the staying power, but their big name is only part of their success. The FTSE 100 index, tracking the UK's 100 largest companies by market value, changed by 14% over the past year alone. Fourteen new companies entered the index and fourteen were excluded during the year. Over three years, the figure is close to 40%. Does that surprise you? In business, things are changing faster all the time, so being the biggest doesn't guarantee anything.

So maybe it is the smaller companies that are capable of being the best thought leaders because they are less restricted by bureaucracy. But then, so many small companies struggle to survive, much less thrive, and it is still only the exceptional ones that rise to the top of mind. You can't really say that just because a company is small, it is going to be innovative. Think about the small companies run by people you know; I'm guessing that most of them could not be classified as 'exceptional'. I believe the conclusion, therefore, is that there is absolutely no correlation between the size of a company and its thought leadership quotient.

A Legend in His Own Mind

You may have met people whose sense of self-importance makes them blind to the fact that other people are not interested or impressed. Simply believing that you are a leader and acting like one will not make it so. It is a good start, however; if you don't believe in yourself and your ideas, then it is very unlikely others will. What annoys me is the attention-seeking, self-aggrandizing boastfulness that wannabe leaders continually thrust upon us, in the hope that we will buy into their myth. There does need to be some substance to the claims, and later on in this book we will go through a number of ways to create and promote yourself with a substantive message.

Imitators and Bullies Beware

Companies that imitate instead of innovate will never be considered thought leaders. At best, they can achieve market leadership, but that will always be based on their ability to copy the next idea, the next trend. Personally I have a lot of respect for companies that take ideas and improve them, learning from the early adopters. However, I have more respect for entrepreneurial spirit and creativity.

Bullying is never an acceptable way to lead. I will not be going into great detail here about the type of bullying that is allowed to go on in our society, from political to corporate, social, racial and other varieties. I just want to be clear that if individuals or organizations are achieving their goals by bullying others, then I do not consider them to be true thought leaders. They may be market leaders, as we said above, but not REAL thought leaders.

Moving ahead at the expense of someone else is never an option. We will go into detail in further chapters as to what makes a REAL thought leader, and you can count on the fact that a high moral standard and personal code of ethics are essential qualities. Just think about what happened in the 2008 U.S. presidential election. As election day grew nearer, both candidates were feeling the stress, but John McCain's team got nasty and started relying on a smear campaign. As the pressure grew, the gap between the candidates also grew, since only one party was playing the smear game and the other was not rising to the bait.

Finally, you can't buy your way to the top. Contrary to popular belief, true thought leadership has little to no correlation to the amount you spend on marketing or advertising.

Cream naturally rises to the top of the milk and REAL thought leaders rise to the top in our communities, businesses, politics and consciousness.

Chapter 2
Thought Leadership is a Choice

"The way to a man's heart is through his opinion."
Steve Forbes

If we have ruled out all the nonsense from the previous chapter, what does a real thought leader look like? How would you go about finding one, or becoming one, if that is of interest? Well, let's start with the Wikipedia definition stated earlier: *'A futurist or person who is recognized among their peers and mentors for innovative ideas and demonstrates the confidence to promote or share those ideas as actionable distilled insights.'* Not bad, but there is one important word missing here: *market*. It's not just about being recognized by your peers and mentors. To effect real change, you need a market, or followers, or fans or constituents or a congregation... you get the idea.

> THOUGHT LEADER: A futurist or person who is recognized among their peers, mentors and market for innovative ideas and demonstrates the confidence to promote and share those ideas as actionable distilled insights.

Sounds simple, doesn't it? The key words I would like us to focus on as we go through the rest of this philosophy are 'recognized', 'innovative ideas' and 'confidence to promote and share'. We need to look at them in a slightly different order, though, because chronologically you would first be innovative, then promote and share your ideas and then, finally, be recognized.

Innovative Ideas

We have already said that change is happening all around us all the time. Our physical bodies, thoughts, the economy, social trends – just about every area of our lives is subject to constant change. However, sometimes big changes are needed, huge shifts that can't wait for the natural evolution of things. Controversial though it was, the multi-billion pound bank bailout of 2008 was one of these big shifts and it took place because the politicians were willing to make bold decisions. The alternative (banks collapsing and people's money disappearing into a black hole) was an unacceptable alternative, so it forced new thinking. Nobel Prize recipient Professor Muhammad Yunus started Grameen Bank with a similar boldness, believing that people in developing countries would be a good risk, and they would pay back micro-loans, if they would just be given the chance and a small investment to start a business. It turned out he was right, and his innovative idea became a model for many other micro-lending programs.

What is New Thinking?

The reason why the term 'thought leadership' is used so sparingly in academic circles is that they (the academics) do not see many people sending out a truly new and unique message. If what you are saying sounds too similar to something else we have heard, then it is not new and will not be counted as thought leadership. There really does have to be a strikingly new angle or idea to be noticed in today's crowded leadership arena. Some say that there are no new ideas, so let me clarify this. It has to *seem* new and different *enough* to get noticed. The idea also has to be disruptive and challenge current views in order to get people's attention. My client Steve Glowinkowski wrote and published the cleverly titled *It's Behaviour, Stupid!* which has attracted many excellent reviews from captains of industry, education and public service. It occurred to me that while the subject of behavior has been studied in various guises, the unique angle Steve takes and the explicit examples of his original framework in real client case studies make the subject easy to understand. It looks at organizational behavior through a new lens, and it seems to be just the kind of lens that people were looking for.

Promoting and Sharing

Being a big fish in a small pond has its advantages. I love running a UK-based business because I have been able to penetrate the market on a broader scale than I would have if I had stayed in the U.S. The UK market is only one-fifth the size of the U.S. market, so it is easier to get one's message across. The smaller geography also helps, since it is easier to travel to different parts of the country. And the media tends to cater for national exposure, with more territory covered by single radio and television stations and print media. Add to that the effect of the internet to cover the entire country and reach international markets, and anyone can make a really big splash.

Anyway, the main objective is to reach a larger, broader audience and become a bit of an icon. I hesitate to use the word 'celebrity' because I lambasted our celebrity culture earlier, and it can have such negative connotations. But we cannot dispute the fact that celebrities certainly do have brand recognition and the power to influence; they attract large sums of money and can create massive change in society. As stated before, one look at people like Bob Geldof, Brad Pitt and Angelina Jolie and Bono, and we see what celebrity can do for important social campaigns.

Positive Change

Everything is constantly changing. In fact, the only constant is change, as Heraclitus famously said. But that does not mean that things change for the better. We won't get too philosophical here and analyze what constitutes 'positive' (because let's face it, a downpour can be seen as very positive after a long period of drought but very unfortunate to a bride whose wedding is taking place outdoors!). Let's assume that most leaders in society act in good faith and want to bring about improvements and progress in their area, and that only a small minority are working with malicious intent.

Positive change can therefore be defined as having a good, desirable and beneficial impact on a person or group of people, or a certain set of circumstances or environment.

In order to improve the chances of positive change, there needs to be a positive intention, which takes more effort. Gandhi, Nelson Mandela, Mother Teresa, Abraham Lincoln and every other leader who has ever created a huge shift in society started with a kernel of an idea and the positive will to make it happen. But these kinds of ideas are all around us, not just in exceptional people. The key is to identify them and give them a chance to shine; in other words, give them a chance to innovate and share their ideas so they can achieve recognition and make a real difference.

One visionary business leader I worked with was at the forefront of email strategy a full ten years before the rest of the population. She wrote an extraordinarily accurate prediction of the ubiquitous email phenomenon in a paper and presented it at a major conference in the mid-1980s. It didn't exactly change the world, but this did not diminish her enthusiasm for the subject. The company began to spread the word about email to clients, giving away software which would allow them to use their personal computers to send messages previously reliant on telex and other slower methods. The culture of the company, being very leading-edge and high-tech, allowed for email communication among staff and, in fact, actively encouraged it. It would have been very easy to stick with older forms of communication; in fact when the computers or software were not behaving, many of us wished we could use the older systems, but the leader led the way with grace and confidence and the customers followed.

Recognition

To be recognized as a leader by one's peers, mentors and the market is an exciting possibility for some people and a scary, daunting one for others. Throughout the rest of this book, we will explore the benefits and the impact of achieving large-scale recognition. We will also look at the inhibitors that prevent most people from attaining it, and, as you might guess, many of them are internal factors that reside in the potential leader himself or herself.

Are You Meant to Be a Thought Leader?

Travelling around the country and internationally, presenting this material, I have been amazed at the level of reluctance and resistance I have faced. It is not just that some leaders don't want to know about it; it is almost like they are fighting for their right to remain non-leaders. Of course I can't name names here (that's a different book), but let's just say that over half of the supposed business leaders I come into contact with are not enthusiastic enough about picking up the full mantle of their job.

Now, before you come after me with your pitchfork, let me say that I do meet amazing business and social leaders who are achieving great things in their organizations. They just don't embody the full 'thought leader' persona that I have described above. The thought leaders will, by definition, always be a select group of people that stand out head and shoulders above their peers. It is simply impossible for too many people to stand out in that way. Think about it. If everyone stood out, no one would stand out.

Excuses, excuses

There is a phrase being uttered in the hallowed halls of the self-development courses these days. It is 'life demands results, not excuses'. Yes, yes, that sounds very good and we see everyone else making excuses all the time, but we don't do that, do we? Here's a thought. Every time you say "I'm too busy", that's an excuse. I'm not saying you are not busy, but when you *mention* your busy-ness to someone else as a reason for not doing something, it's an excuse. I can't see it any other way. Sam Silverstein, recent President of the National Speakers Association, runs a company called No More Excuses. His definition of an excuse is a lie we tell ourselves to deceive ourselves and others. Real thought leaders are not interested in making excuses because they are too busy going after their vision. Real thought leaders are out there changing the world while others are still asleep.

Pressure of Time

If you want a job done, give it to a busy person. You may have heard that expression before; it's one of my favorites. But did you know that when you translate that into executive mode, the result is exponential? Studies have shown that executives typically put in more hours and get more accomplished than average workers. So why would they be the ideal candidates for additional work? It's simple. The pressure of time encourages the busy executive to find more and more creative ways of getting more and more done. They get better at delegating; they get faster at decision-making.

> Real thought leaders are out there changing the world while others are still asleep.

Thomas Power, chairman of social networking community Ecademy, is one of the 'busiest' people I know, yet he gets an amazing amount done in an average week. He reads more books than most other people I meet (and not by speed-reading either), he meets people in person, maintains email and blog exchanges, meets people face-to-face and always seems to be creating new projects and getting involved in something. He also manages to play tennis on a regular basis and spend time with his family. What's his secret? I believe he makes fast decisions and doesn't waste time.

"A man who dares to waste one hour of time has not discovered the value of life." - Charles Darwin

REAL Thought Leaders Tackle the Important as well as the Urgent

All the best time managers talk about four quadrants where we tend to spend our time. The quadrants are formed by using two axes – one for Importance and the other for Urgency. Quadrant Three is Urgent but Not Important. These are things like reading emails marked 'Urgent', answering the telephone and other fire-fighting activities.

Quadrant Two is Important but Not Urgent. These are things that will help us achieve our longer-term goals and usually represent areas of growth and major achievement. This is the area where in my opinion that we do not spend enough time and focus. We allow ourselves to react and constantly deal with the Urgent items because they are usually easier to achieve quickly, while the non-Urgent tasks are not pressing enough. But long-term, if we don't spend at least some time on the Important tasks, they never get done.

Think about the big goals you have had over the years: losing weight, starting a business, writing a book. How many times did the big (arguably more important) goal go on the back burner or get postponed because you chose to do less important things?

If you have Important goals, you need to carve out the time to work on those as well as the Urgent items; go to that higher plane for a few minutes each day or each week and you will see the big picture starting to come into sharper focus and your life starting to become the masterpiece that you designed. One of the best strategies my clients use to guarantee focus on their important jobs is to remove distractions and annoyances, at least temporarily. This usually involves turning the mobile phone to off (not silent, since flashing or vibrating could interrupt you), working offline so there are no emails or other messages arriving unexpectedly, or even working off-site. I am currently sitting in a café as I write this, my phone is turned off and I have purposely not connected to the internet. It can wait. It can all wait, I promise.

REAL Thought Leadership is a Choice

After all I have just explained, if you don't feel ready, able, willing or happy about being a thought leader, then don't! It's as simple as that. By definition, we can't have a world full of leaders anyway. There have to be some people left to do the following. The last thing I want to do is force anyone to step up and out of their comfort zone to do something they don't want to do anyway.

If you are still undecided, I applaud your honesty. Read to the end of the book, get clear on the requirements of a thought leader, ask yourself the difficult questions and then decide.

Too many people lead their lives feeling largely unfulfilled. When lack of fulfilment comes from ignoring or fighting the voice inside that has something important to say, the feeling is magnified. My mission in life is to encourage and support people with important views and opinions to share, and to make sure they do it well, do it effectively and easily, and most importantly, do it in the right way for them.

Chapter 3
REAL Thought Leadership

Real thought leadership is rare and highly desirable. New and innovative thinking has propelled our society over many thousands of years, yet it is always a handful of people who come to mind. What attributes make up a thought leader? As mentioned previously, innovation scores pretty highly. But as with every kind of leader, not much happens until there is a following of some kind. Thought leaders influence others' thinking, which leads to action which in turn creates shifts in society.

> **Everyone has in them the potential to be a revolutionary thinker and there is *no limit* to the number of great thinkers we can accommodate.**

Is thought leadership really so rare? As I said, the common perception is that one needs to have truly revolutionary ideas to be considered a thought leader. That may or may not be true. I have seen people do incredible things just by thinking *slightly* differently from the crowd. Tony Robbins talks about the power of a two-millimeter shift. Imagine you are in your car, driving along the road. What would happen if you shifted the steering wheel of your car just two millimeters to the left? If you left it in that position for just a few seconds, the car would start going towards the left and would end up turning a lot more than two millimeters – and you would probably cause an accident.

My personal view is that everyone has in them the potential to be a revolutionary thinker and there is *no limit* to the number of great thinkers we can accommodate. The issue is how we define it.

Over the past ten years, I have worked with many amazing individuals who saw themselves as leaders in their fields. Not only that, but they are recognized by their peers and their customers as true leaders. There's a kind of consensus about what defines a leader and it is certainly not my intention to cover that ground here. However, to get to the next step that I was describing above, that cordoned-off area called 'real thought leadership', several things must be in place.

Many of the authors I have worked with over this time have been visionary leaders, and they have taught me more about real thought leadership than any textbook I have read. During the process of planning and creating writing strategies, books and articles, I have been through the ups and downs with them, exploring their thinking and their creativity, their goals and their worries, their successes and their learnings.

Four Key Attributes of a REAL Thought Leader

The hundred or so attributes fell into four logical areas, and the more I thought about it, the more sense it made. I started to share this concept with audiences and clients about a year ago and they gave me resounding feedback that I was on the right track. The four attributes give a context and a framework to achieve the three objectives outlined in our earlier definition: innovative ideas, promoting and sharing and recognition. They enable us to measure and assess thought leaders more accurately and precisely. And perhaps most importantly, they provide the 'how': a roadmap with specific instructions for aspiring thought leaders to follow that will help them reach their goal. A focus on these four attributes can literally move someone from being an excellent leader to being perceived as a real thought leader. And in the busy lives of our clients, in a crowded marketplace, the real thought leaders will rise to the top and take the limelight and the business. It's only natural.

> **The four attributes give a context and a framework to achieve the three objectives outlined in our earlier definition: innovative ideas, promoting and sharing, and recognition.**

The four attributes conveniently create an acronym that spells R-E-A-L, which makes it easy to remember, doesn't it? But don't let the cuteness of this acronym distract you from the very solid advice and implications I'm offering you. If you follow the formula, you can achieve a position of REAL thought leadership in your field and in the greater community or society, if you so choose.

The acronym R–E–A–L stands for:

R	=	Reach
E	=	Engagement
A	=	Authority
L	=	Longevity

With these four things in place, you will be able to innovate, share your ideas and become the recognized 'thought leader' in your field. As we go through each of them in detail, you will see not only how they each play unique and specific roles, but also how they work together to create an overall result.

Do you need all of them to be considered a thought leader? Not necessarily. But if you look at the strategies, successes and significance of people whom you consider to be thought leaders, you rarely find only one of these qualities. Picture a chair with four legs. The chair is very stable because the weight is balanced evenly on the four legs. Remove one leg and it may start to wobble. Remove two of the legs and you would not want to sit down too hard on that chair. Take off three of the legs and you will probably find yourself sitting on a hard floor! With the REAL acronym, you have four legs or four chances to be successful. Use them all.

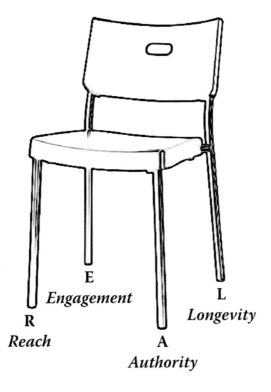

E
Engagement

L
Longevity

R
Reach

A
Authority

It is possible to use only one attribute and still gain a significant advantage over people who don't have that attribute. But you wouldn't want to rely on just one. Think about it. You may have noticed people trying to achieve their goals by using just one strategy. Let's say a business owner puts all of their focus and attention on extending their reach without working on engagement. How successful would they be? Equally, if you know someone who is a true authority on their subject, but they are only known within a tiny circle of influence, how much impact could he or she really have?

The reason why the chair falls over when it has only one or two legs is that there is too much pressure on those legs. I liken this to companies that are inflexible and use the same strategies over and over, even when the market is changing, and they are not getting the results they once were. The debacle of General Motors is simply astounding. A big established company like that could have, and should have, implemented key changes to its processes well before it needed a government bailout with only weeks to spare. Solid, confident leadership should have ensured new approaches, new strategies and a successful future for a company at the heart of American industry.

The Rules of the Game

If you are going to play a game, you need to know the rules. It is no different with leadership in general, or thought leadership in particular. Simply having a benchmark and measurement criteria give you something to aim for and keep yourself on track. Knowing what the four attributes are gives you a tremendous advantage over other people who may be running around in the wrong direction. The rules are there to keep some kind of order, and they also offer the ability to determine who wins the game. As I mentioned earlier, more than one person can win the gold medal in this game; in fact there can be many winners. But there should never be any disputes about who is winning the game because the REAL thought leaders (or winners) will be judged fairly and accurately.

Just One Last Word on Fairness

The losers of this world complain that life isn't fair. What they don't realize (but you and I do) is that it is not the hand you are dealt that counts, but how you play it. Life may not be fair but, in a democratic society, once you get into the game of REAL thought leadership, if you play fairly you will receive fair treatment and a fair chance. I think that's great.

What is unfair is having to play a game without knowing the rules. Having others decide whether you win or lose and sometimes changing the rules halfway through the game – that's extremely unfair and I can see why people sometimes don't want to play. In the game of REAL thought leadership, the four attributes are immutable principles, not something vague, trendy or shifting on a whim. The rules have always been there; they just haven't always been shared with the players. And now they have, so may the best leaders win!

Chapter 4
Reach for the BOLD

Isn't it amazing how we all know about the top people in business, politics, philosophy, the arts and many other fields, even if they are in different countries? As I've said, we have the internet to thank for the speed and breadth of information at our fingertips, and we also want to acknowledge those who are working the publicity machine to let us know about them. I know quite a few people who are experts in their little area, and yet they don't have the brand recognition or the market penetration that they could have. Does it matter? If no one knows about them, what good is their expertise and how much impact can they really have? But I have to reiterate here that it only matters if they feel unfulfilled and dissatisfied with their results. There is nothing wrong with being a small fish in a small pond. However, to achieve positive change and influence larger groups will usually require a bigger and bolder plan.

Good Reasons to Extend Your Reach

I would like you to consider becoming a household name. Can you imagine how it would feel to be known by all of the prospective clients that need to know about you? Would it help you achieve your business and personal goals a bit faster? You could also command higher fees if the demand on your time were greater than the time you had available. People will pay more to work with the thought leaders of this world.

It's not just about the money, though, is it? When we feel passionately about our subject and have something important to share, we want the whole world to know about it. I can't tell you how many times aspiring authors have said to me that the most important thing for them is to get their book into as many hands as possible. They usually add that it's not about the money, but, as we said before, there is nothing wrong with that. The main goal, however, is to reach lots of people, to touch lots of lives. That passion and desire to share something important drives people to do a lot more towards extending their reach than the goal of the money alone.

Extending reach is usually seen as a job for Marketing and PR but it is not solely the responsibility of Marketing to extend the reach of your company. As head of your business, you need to be involved. No, scratch that. You need to *own* the job of extending reach and do whatever is necessary to make sure your addressable market knows about you and your products and services. I have seen too many cases of top executives abdicating their responsibility in this area and then blaming the marketing department or the PR company when things do not go as well as expected. Conversely, with good direction from senior leaders, the PR company and the marketing department can finally do their best work and execute on the vision.

How far can you extend your reach? Let's consider this in the literal sense and then look at a few other ways you can do it.

Geography

Geographic reach is the obvious one that springs to mind. Creating larger markets and growing the customer base is a basic goal of business. About half of the business people I meet each year have goals of extending into new territories, many of them international. There is a certain excitement about going beyond one's own borders and becoming known and successful in a new place.

My friend and client Roy Palmer is an expert in human physiology and a qualified teacher of the Alexander Technique. He has developed a reputation as a real authority in this field by working with some of the British sports teams, especially the cricket team. With his second book *Zone Mind, Zone Body*, Roy started to get noticed in the North American market, which led not only to book sales but professional opportunities as well. Roy now sells more books in the U.S. than in his native UK market; considering the size of the U.S., the potential is enormous.

> Widespread appeal depends on getting through to more than just your immediate peer group or obvious market.

Roy's expansion into North America was an added bonus. Many authors consciously plan their entrée into new markets by promoting books in those markets and speaking there. Carol Talbot is a very successful NLP trainer based in

Dubai. Originally from the UK, Carol now focuses on the local market in Dubai, but her book *Hitting the Wall... and Breaking Through* gives her visibility in many other markets. She also worked with a UK PR firm to gain even more exposure in Europe.

I love working with people in different countries. In addition to challenging me to create the best products and services, it also makes me feel more exotic and interesting than I already am. I also find it fun and exciting to work with people from different cultures and it feeds a basic human need for variety. Other entrepreneurs I know have chosen not to go for geographic expansion for family or economic reasons, or just because of personal preference.

How about you? Is a greater geographic reach one of your goals?

Cross-cultural and Other Factors

Geographic reach is not the only criterion for success. You can be an exemplary leader in your business and industry, even if you limit your market to your own town or city, or your church or even your neighborhood. People create change every day in little pockets of our society. However, I think that when you find someone creating massive changes, that person has usually managed to cut across several segments of society: age, gender, religion, education and many more. Widespread appeal depends on getting through to more than just your immediate peer group or obvious market.

Be Relevant

There is no point extending your reach as a business writer

to people who don't read business books and magazines. You won't be noticed as an architect by people who have no desire to build or extend a building. If someone has not got a toothache, they are generally not thinking about finding a dentist. I'm sure you get the picture.

Reg Athwal has been building a successful career as a world-class business speaker for many years. He is a recognized expert in entrepreneurship and human resources, whose mission in life is to help people discover, identify and unleash their talent. Lately his conversations have bubbled over with enthusiasm for his new venture OneTVO, an exciting internet television concept that will ultimately bring hundreds of top-quality business programs to viewers in over 24 countries. When we met in Dubai earlier this year, we discussed how to position his two businesses to ensure that the new one does not distract or confuse clients who book him to speak. It turns out that the television company is completely complementary and relevant; it is simply another medium to add to the mix, one that does not conflict with his writing and speaking, as long as the message is always clear.

Sector-specific Reach

Moving into New Sectors

Going beyond your normal market sometimes means getting out of your comfort zone. A client of mine had spent a number of years working exclusively with individual business owners and entrepreneurs and he was beginning to get a bit complacent. He knew he needed to up his game and get into larger accounts, but it was easy to keep doing what he'd always done. It was only when times got tougher that he forced himself to extend his reach and go after the bigger fish. Moving into new sectors is a strategic decision and it normally requires resources of time, money and effort, so it should be undertaken with careful thought.

Narrowing Down to One Sector to Extend Reach within that Sector

The power of niching is just starting to hit home for a lot of people I know. My own story is a classic niching success story. In 2002, I was running a marketing consultancy business with book coaching as one strand of it. Gradually I found that my passion and interest for creating good books with clients overtook the rest of my projects. It was a huge decision to give up the other work, and it did hurt to say no to non-core projects in order to focus on books. In the first few months after making that decision, I wavered and nearly jumped back several times into broader marketing roles. However, I had a strong desire to focus and deliver one thing really well.

A few years later, I found I could no longer support aspiring authors of fiction because that did not fit well enough into the methodology and process I was developing. My real passion was for business and personal development books and I felt I could do a better job for those clients. Again, it was hard to say no and I wondered if it would impact the business negatively. Just the opposite, as it turns out. The number of enquiries into the business (most of them precisely the profile of clients I target) has grown exponentially, aided by the other REAL thought leavdership strategies I am sharing with you in this book. When you are willing to go deep and narrow into a niche, you can become known as the real thought leader within that niche and achieve that recognition from a smaller but very relevant group.

Redefining a Sector

Apple, one of the few *companies* that I might be willing to call a 'thought leader', has gone from being a computer manufacturer suited to designers and other artistic types to a ubiquitous, leading-edge provider of information and entertainment devices appealing to many types of consumers. One could argue that they are still favored by the younger generation but even that is changing. My mother, who is in her late sixties, has an iPod now and knows how to put music onto it. We have at least three or four iPods in our household. The top executives at Apple decided to make a big play for the broad consumer market and no one can argue with the success of the iPod and the iPhone. They chose to go wide as their leadership is already in quite a narrow range of products. Interestingly, the Mac is still a major product for Apple, but it is now part of the blended home/work/ entertainment proposition that appeals to a specific type of person.

You Have a Choice to Make

"The great thing in the world is not so much where we stand, as in what direction we are moving."
- Oliver Wendell Holmes

Do you want to go deep or wide? Will you extend your reach further into the geographic and cultural markets as discussed above, or will you extend your reach deeper into your existing market? Will you redefine what you offer, or the market you serve? Ultimately, the decision will be made according to your business goals and personal aspirations.

How to Achieve Greater Reach

There are so many ways to achieve greater reach that I almost don't know where to begin. Marketing textbooks dedicate hundreds of pages to expound on this theme. That is because if you want to increase business and your reputation as a REAL thought leader, it is all about marketing. This should be part of your strategic plan.

I would like you to focus on a few key areas where you can have a big impact in a short time.

Effective Networking

For four years, I managed several chapters of BNI, the largest and arguably the most successful referral organization in the world. The purpose of the groups was to create an environment where members could get to know other business people, build trust and feel comfortable referring their clients. In return, if they presented their business effectively, they would receive referrals as well. I started three of those groups with my own bare hands and that gave me the opportunity to influence a large number of people on a weekly basis about how to network effectively. I also ran training courses for members and continue to do so for business organizations that need to understand how to include networking in a serious marketing or thought leadership strategy.

Extending reach, for many people, means building a larger list of contacts. Busy business leaders often have good lists of contacts they have built over time, but the challenge can be meeting new people. Ironically, the more successful the business becomes, the more important it is to continue building the contacts but, of course, the more challenging it becomes in terms of time. Having joined Ecademy as a BlackStar life member, I made a long-term commitment to meet people and get to know them. However, during extremely successful periods in my business, I have been known to 'drop off the face of the earth' and I have seen other colleagues do the same. It seems like a good excuse: too much business. The problem is that when you are not networking or otherwise reminding people about you, then you are not visible. Out of sight, out of mind. Basically, people may forget about you, especially if your competitors are still out there networking. As we mentioned earlier, people are busier than ever and bombarded with marketing messages, emails and just sheer volume of information.

You Need to have a Constant Visibility Strategy

The one point I do want to get across is that great leaders have always used networking to their advantage and, even though the personality of networking may look different, the necessary strategies are still the same. Online networking has many advantages in terms of time savings and travel savings, but you have to admit that the dynamic is not the same as 'in person'. Visionary thought leaders have a strategy for both, so let's look at the top things they do.

The Elevator Pitch or How to Get Your Best Message Across

Once you have decided which events to attend, you need to think about what you are going to say when you are asked that question. You know the one: "What do you do?" It sounds innocent enough but it can turn the most eloquent and intelligent business person into a babbling idiot. So Rule Number One is 'less is more'. You will need a clever-sounding elevator pitch that lasts about 60 seconds (for those events where you are given exactly 60 seconds to tell people what you do). In addition to that, I would strongly recommend putting together one sentence that encapsulates the essence of your product or service, plus the value that you personally bring to the table. Most people make the mistake of only talking about their products and that is a huge mistake. If you have difficulty explaining your expertise in one sentence, you may need to do some ground work on your proposition. A great person to help you would be my friend Richard White, founder of The Accidental Salesman®. In a recent discussion with Richard, we agreed that the majority of people do not articulate their value well enough or concisely enough. We will cover this in much more detail in the following two chapters.

Meeting the Right People

Many inexperienced networkers confuse networking with selling. Those of us who are passionate about this area believe it is more about meeting people and deciding if there are any potential areas of common ground, any reason to get to know them better. Business may follow at a later date. The people you meet may not even be in your target market, but they may know other people who are. You simply don't know; that's why you must keep an open mind.

How many People do you Need in Your Network?

With the advent of Facebook and Twitter, it can seem like it is a numbers game. I believe that the people who treat it that way will never reap the true rewards of networking, which have to do with building trust among people you know and like. It can be tricky to get the same kind of value from an online experience that you would in person, and it may be tempting just to build a large list. Andy Lopata, a fellow speaker and recognized networking guru, suggests that you do not simply look to connect people to add to your 'notches on the bedpost'. He says, "A request to connect should contain a reason to do so, a line of greeting and an explanation of what you might have in common. After all, would you approach someone at a networking event and simply say 'let's exchange business cards' before walking off?"

The quality is infinitely more important than the quantity, in this case. Some entrepreneurial contacts of mine have had tremendous success with just a handful of clients and contacts.

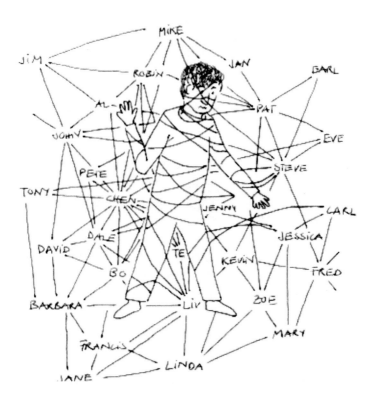

Continuously Educate and Promote to Your Network

When you meet people at networking events or even online, it should not be a one-time experience. The first meeting is a chance for you to see whether there could be any interesting conversations to have in the future. You should be looking to meet new people all the time, and pursue discussions with them in between events. Dave Clarke, one of the founders of lunchtime networking leader NRG, recently identified a major mistake many networkers make. He noticed people attending many events and meeting hundreds of people, as if the goal were to simply collect the business cards. Ironically, they are getting overwhelmed by trying to remember and keep up with the sheer numbers of people they are meeting, and it is causing them stress.

We've heard people say they don't want to attend a networking event because they can't handle any more contacts. Sometimes, Dave says, we get so busy meeting new people that we forget to cultivate the relationships with the people we already know. That's crazy, when you think about the fact that it is the people with whom you have developed real trust that are most likely to do business with you or refer you to other clients. Dave is also the person who inspired me to develop my 'inner network' of advocates, the small group of very loyal and trusted people who I know very well and who know me very well. This is a chapter about extending your reach, but that does not mean that you neglect the deeper relationships.

Writing and Publishing

Of all the marketing strategies that exist, writing and publishing is the best way to achieve greater reach.

Well, I *would* say that, wouldn't I? But it's true. And I'm not the only one saying it. If you want to get known, you absolutely must be writing and publishing. How else could you get your message out to as many people as possible? As we have just seen, networking is an important part of your marketing strategy, but imagine if all you could do was talk to people in person. Even if you spoke to large groups, it would still take a long time to reach your market. Professional speakers know that they need books to extend their reach. (Please note that when I use the word 'book', many times it is a metaphor for all the possible means of getting your message across.)

> **If you want to get known, you absolutely must be writing and publishing.**

Anthony Robbins has achieved most of his following from people who have read his book and listened to his tapes. Many years after original publication, the bestselling *Awaken The Giant Within* continues to sell well and attract people to his live events. *The Secret*, in book form and DVD, spread the message about the Law of Attraction widely and rapidly, giving many of the experts showcased a huge new market and household name status. Most business people I know had *not* heard of Dr. John Demartini or Bob Proctor before *The Secret*, despite the fact that those experts were speaking to thousands of people every year for many years. With books and other products, great leaders with innovative ideas can be instantly catapulted into the mass market.

Think about the bestselling business books over the past few years, books like The *One Minute Manager*, *Good to Great*, *The Tipping Point*, *The E-Myth Revisited*. How many of those authors could have achieved such a level of popularity and recognition without having a book? It certainly would have taken a lot longer without the book.

Remember, there may be people who will never get to hear you speak in a live environment. They may live too far away, have financial constraints or physical challenges preventing them from attending your talks. And there simply aren't enough hours in the day to speak to the whole market in person! The only way you will be able to reach these people is with your books – and remember, when I say 'book', please read 'products'. So many clients tell me of the excitement they feel when they get fan mail and book reviews from clients in new markets, many of whom they will never meet in person.

Perhaps you are the one who cannot travel, or maybe you choose not to travel that much. A lot of working mothers I know choose to minimize the amount they travel because it cuts into family time. I myself think twice before committing to out-of-town engagements.

More extreme cases include speakers and authors who have physical restrictions such as illnesses or incapacitation. Sue Chambers is an amazing woman who has suffered with multiple sclerosis (MS) for over twenty years. She wrote her book to share her story and her perspective on keeping a sense of humor and positive attitude no matter what life throws at you. Sue is wheelchair-bound and tires easily. She wants her book, her audio book and her video material to be out there working for her when she cannot go in person. *Magical Sense* has the capacity to work for Sue and enlighten people about MS twenty-four hours a day, seven days a week, in different markets, without Sue exhausting herself!

If you are a speaker, you have some very good reasons to think about reach. Imagine a scenario where someone hears you speak and buys a book. After reading it, the person could then give your book to his friend. Now you have reached someone else who has never met you and may never get to meet you. The possibilities are endless. The best result is when the book gets into the hands of someone who has the potential to invite you to speak. All professional speakers have heard that they need to have a book. A book can help the speaker's business in countless ways, including reinforcing the material from presentations and going beyond the talk into more advanced information. However, the strongest reason of all for a speaker to write and publish is to extend their reach quickly.

Print and Online

When we talk about writing and publishing, we should consider print and online. Do you already have a complete writing and publishing strategy which includes both print and online materials?

You should have blogs, articles, books and ebooks in your plan because each one has a different purpose and each one needs to be handled in a slightly different way. In addition, they all need to support each other and reinforce what the other materials are doing. Very often, I will start working with a business professional who wants to bring out a book as soon as possible, and we find there is scope to do a lot more than just one book. One of my favorite projects involved creating the messaging for a full-length printed book, a series of ebooks, a large series of articles, blogs (yes, these were planned and part of the strategy!) as well as the speaking engagements that the client needed to deliver.

All Books are NOT Created Equal

The great thing about books is that they can carry your message to the far reaches of your market, across the country and across the globe. Ebooks in particular have become very popular because of the information focus and the ease of download. The main purpose of an ebook is to deliver a specific chunk of information that solves a particular business problem. But if you think that you will become a REAL thought leader just by producing ebooks, have another think.

An ebook is not necessarily just an electronic version of a printed book! Nor is it simply a shorter version of a book. That is a total cop-out and when I hear people saying that they plan to produce an ebook instead of a printed book, I always check that they are not just being lazy. Sometimes they are trying to avoid the cost and delay of getting their book into print. When you compare an ebook with its counterpart in print, however, it would always be better to have the book in print. It certainly creates more credibility.

I don't know about you, but I've seen a lot of really terrible ebooks over the past few years. Ebooks which promised the world and delivered nothing. I even have some I have never read, still sitting in a folder on my computer. What makes it worse is that ebooks tend to attract higher prices, allegedly because of the ability to download them instantly, but I believe it is just a cultural phenomenon which we have allowed to take hold. $97 for a 45-page ebook when the print version would have a price tag of about $19.99? Who are we kidding?! This trend of overpriced ebooks has got to stop. It reminds me of *The Emperor's New Clothes*. No one wants to admit that ebooks are overpriced. Those people who do buy them do so mainly because of the copy on lengthy sales pages promising many secrets that will be revealed. Sometimes they are disappointed.

Luckily, the real potential of ebooks has just started to surface. The ebook *can* be an electronic version of a book in print. New ebook readers are entering the market (especially in the U.S.) with good features that make books easy to read. The main benefit is the weight of the device, allowing you to have access to a thousand books in the palm of your hand, as opposed to the heavy printed versions. For travellers facing increasingly strict baggage restrictions, it's an appealing proposition. But I believe the hard copy book in print is here to stay for quite some time, and it can achieve things the electronic version will never achieve.

The book in print is so much higher up the pecking order in terms of credibility and perceived value that I can't even compare the two with a straight face. You don't often hear business leaders boasting about being the author of ebooks and, if they did, they wouldn't be taken as seriously as the author of a book in print. I think it's because we know what goes into the book in print and normally that is a lot more time, effort, thought and care.

> In short, only a printed book can help you achieve your goals of credibility and authority.

Imagine going to see a prospective client and handing him a copy of your book, which you have signed. Feel the weight of it in your hands and the smoothness of the cover. Now imagine yourself handing the book over to your client and his expression as he looks at the front cover, then the back cover, then flicks through the pages and smiles at a phrase or two. You know what he is thinking of you: "This person knows what he is talking about and has put together a very impressive book on the subject."

Now try to imagine the same scenario with your ebook. You don't hand it over to your client; you attach it to an email and it goes into the client's overcrowded Inbox. Do you think he will even find time to open the attachment? If he does, what will be his reaction? Not exactly the same as the printed book scenario. Besides, the printed book will be personally signed by you!

In short, only a printed book can help you achieve your goals of credibility and authority.

It is a bit short-sighted nowadays to consider just writing and publishing one book, when the market demands so much more. You would just be leaving opportunities on the table. The electronic version, as we've just seen, is becoming more popular.

However, the print version is so important that I have dedicated a whole chapter to it. If, even after my arguments for putting a book into the market to raise your profile and gain the status of a REAL thought leader, you really do not want to write a book, then you can simply skip that chapter.

Why You Should Be Speaking in Public

If you are already convinced that speaking is an important way for a leader to get his/her message into the world, or you are very enthusiastic about speaking, you may skip this section. If, on the other hand, you are not happy about doing public speaking, or have any fears about it at all, you need to read this section before moving on.

Speaking is a natural way to assert your position as an authority on your topic. It never ceases to amaze me how some business leaders are excited about it and want to speak to as many audiences as possible, the larger the better, while others are dragged on to the platform kicking and screaming by their shareholders, communications department or PR agency. I have many friends in the professional speaking world who do it because they love it. If you watch someone who loves the platform, you tend to think of them as a 'good speaker', but this is not necessarily true.

The most important ingredients for success as a speaker are a clear message and an absolute passion and conviction for getting that message across to audiences that need to hear it.

We will discuss how to develop a clear message in Chapter 6, so for now just trust that you have one, or will have one soon. How about your passion and conviction? How is that doing on a scale of one to ten? Go on, give yourself a mental score before we move on.

The less-than-enthusiastic would-be speakers I meet generally have a lower passion or conviction around their subject. I will never forget an executive I used to work with coming up with multiple excuses and reasons for not doing speaking engagements. I was one of the corporate communications 'nags' at the time, so my main objective was to get him in front of customers and sharing the company's leading-edge thinking and philosophy. It turned out that he was not one hundred percent convinced about the company's position as a leader in the industry; therefore his own role was not attached to a solid enough foundation.

The best speakers I see, be they corporate executives or entrepreneurs, have a rock-solid belief in themselves, their organization and their key messages. Luckily we will be discussing key messages at length in Chapter 6.

How Speaking and Writing Complement Each Other

Your books, articles and speaking are all just different ways of getting your message out to your target market. They should all convey the same message and, in fact, complement each other so that if your market sees any of your products, it knows it's one of yours.

There's nothing like speaking to really see the impact you make. I hope you like instant feedback because you will get it when you speak in public. Firstly, you will get the body language of the audience. Then you will see if people are willing to interact with you, answer your questions or ask questions of their own. Finally, if you get them to fill in feedback forms, you will know very quickly what kind of job you did.

Compare this to traditional writing, where you sometimes get book reviews or write-ups on your material. The advent of the internet has created a lot more interaction between authors and their market. For example, people can comment on your blog, forward an email, click through to other products and articles and much more.

> **I hope you like instant feedback because you will get it when you speak in public**.

When you add speaking to the mix, you can get a variety of feedback, verbal and written, to help you continuously refine your message and delivery.

Another Idea: Video

If you really don't like the idea of delivering live presentations, you can make some videos in the comfort of your own home or office, and upload those on to the internet. Video is fast becoming an acceptable and almost expected medium for communication. If you are willing to get your videos professionally recorded and edited, that will put you in the best possible light. One way or another, you need to get your message heard by more people or you will never achieve the reach you need.

Many leaders I know have started to use video proactively to communicate with their customers. It is simply another medium to reach people, complementing emails, blogs, live events, books and articles.

How Often is Often Enough?

You establish your authority by having something to say and by saying it at the right intervals. There is no need to annoy your customers with overly frequent communications. The right frequency will depend on so many factors, but primarily the tolerance of your target market and the rate at which information changes in your industry.

Take just as much care, if not more, in planning your video communications as you do with your written ones. It can be a lot easier to be spontaneous when speaking, and many people go off on tangents. They are also usually less rigorous with their language than when they write. Ensure that there is a consistent message, style, tone and personality throughout all of your communications – written, spoken or even on video.

Chapter 5
Good Engagement is BOLD

What is Engagement?

Engagement involves a heart-to-heart connection with your client, customer, audience or reader. It is based on two parties having similar values, and operating under an umbrella of mutual trust and respect. Thought leaders need to project this trust and respect first, in order to have it returned to them. Is it strange to see the word 'heart' in a business book? I have seen the word being used more often recently because our society is changing. Folks are realizing once again that people do business with people. I think for a while we may have forgotten that

Think about your own interactions with employees, clients, affiliates, shareholders, other stakeholders. Think about the level of engagement that you are willing to allow in those relationships. When we hold back and we don't engage or we engage at the level that we feel 'appropriate', we only get a limited result. Real thought leaders push the boundaries and go beyond what is expected; they go way beyond what their competitors offer.

Engagement is one of those woolly areas that you can't quite put your arms around. You can't really measure it, can you? However, we still need to focus on it so we can improve things where possible. When everything else is equal, engagement can be the key to winning deals and success in business.

Think of one person with whom you deal in business; it doesn't matter who it is; the first person that comes to mind. Think about that relationship. What would you like to achieve with that relationship that you are not achieving now? Chances are, it has something to do with engagement. Maybe you are not on the same wavelength. Maybe they want more of a personal relationship with you; or perhaps you are the one who would value the personal relationship but they are keeping you at arm's length.

Ask yourself, "What would happen if I pushed that boundary out a bit, if I just created more engagement within that one relationship with that one person?" Then ask yourself how you could achieve it.

Engagement is also a two-way street. Your customers and clients want to engage with you, and with all the communications tools available to them now, such as email, mobile phones, blogs, communities and the like, they expect to find you and enter into a conversation with you.

You are the one reading this book so you are the one who is in control of the relationship at the moment. Hopefully you will get some ideas so that you can at least keep up with customer demands, and ideally get one step ahead of them.

When someone takes the time to read your book or listen to you speak, they are engaging with you. Etiquette and common sense would dictate that you engage with

them in the right way or you risk alienating them. The worst offense, in my opinion, is a superior or condescending tone. I hate being lectured at, don't you? Not only is it an old-fashioned way to get a message across, but it is seen as rude nowadays. Sadly, some managers still employ this type of communication when speaking to their subordinates and I will give them the benefit of the doubt because they probably don't know about the techniques I am about to share with you.

Step One: Define the Right Audience or Target Market

So many business leaders are actually very bad at describing their target market. They either think that 'everyone' is potentially a client, or they focus on the type of clients they have been working with historically. Most business people I meet – and I meet thousands of them every year – are hopelessly vague or clueless in this area.

I want you to be better than that. I would like you to approach this the way we have been approaching the rest of your thought leadership strategy: in a conscious and strategic way. This means you need to put some time into it, and maybe get the help of a business or marketing consultant. Once you are clear about your audience, all kinds of things are possible, such as a profound understanding of their characteristics, needs, pain and goals. You will also be able to tailor your message more accurately to suit them, so that it resonates with them and they feel confident that you do understand them. This will result in a better return on your efforts.

Now let's look at how to achieve the best relationship with the people you have decided to target.

Posture

Your mother or your teacher may have lectured you on your posture. That is not what I'm talking about here. Another type of posture I'd like you to consider is that of your speech. There are different ways of speaking to people and you can probably see that if you approach your communication with this in mind, you can improve the effectiveness of that communication and, hence, your success in general.

Superior

This is the posture described above, where the manager talked down to his subordinates. Even using a word like 'subordinates' designates a superior-inferior relationship, and that is exactly how it is perceived by the listener.

Posture has a huge role to play in written materials. When writing things like articles, blogs and books, it is absolutely critical to create the right tone. If you lecture at people, they will be turned off and you won't even have the chance to explain yourself because you are not there in person.

The superior posture can be used in a positive way with great effect, when you need to assert your authority on a particular subject. It also comes in handy when dealing with nay-sayers, hecklers and other 'problem people'. I just don't recommend it as the primary mode of communication if you are trying to build relationships with people.

Equal

It's fun to treat people as equals. The most common reference for equal relationships is among friends so you are, in effect, using the strategies you use (probably unconsciously) in a friendship. The nature of this posture is putting someone at ease, finding similarities and common goals. You can get into this posture very easily by using the word 'we' and speaking about shared situations and experiences.

Another excellent place to come from an equal posture is in networking situations. We have discussed networking briefly, and it will come up again in a later chapter. However, the emphasis here is not *if* or *why* you should network, but *how* to network. If you see networking the way I do, and the way some of the top networking consultants I know see it, the goal is to build relationships and trust. You will be having hundreds of networking conversations this year and I would like you to consider having those conversations from an equal standpoint. After all, you are in the same room, in the same community, in the same boat, if you will. You have similar objectives as the person with whom you are speaking.

Find common ground, engage in a little harmless industry gossip, share useful tips that have helped you in your business. Anything to put you on an equal footing and to avoid 'selling' which usually comes from a superior posture.

Inferior

You can also achieve wonderful things by using an inferior posture. There are some things that your clients know more about than you do, so you can acknowledge that and make them feel good. I'm not talking about false gratification or flattery; you have to find real examples of their superior knowledge. For example, they would be more knowledgeable about the customer experience with your company than you would, right? I became aware of this communications strategy several years ago and every time I use it, I get very positive results. Again, I can't emphasise enough that it needs to be totally accurate and authentic, not false, or the customer will see through it.

People whose communication is mostly one-sided miss opportunities to engage and they may not realize how valuable that could be. I had a meeting with a business consultant a few months ago and he was obviously very full of himself. He spent hours talking about how great he was and all the great work he did. Then, almost as an afterthought, he asked about me. I had not managed to get one full sentence out about my business projects when he proceeded to interrupt me every few seconds with even more stories of his supposed expertise! Needless to say, I didn't feel inclined to send him any business because I simply don't like the way he treats people.

"Enough about me; now let me tell you about myself."

We all know people like this. People who do not even try to build a good relationship with us and perhaps they don't care. Or perhaps they just don't know the secrets.

True engagement is like a seduction. It starts out slowly and builds, using more 'pull' than push. Think about the last time you seduced someone, or were seduced by someone. There is a certain mystery and intrigue about it, an inherent excitement in not knowing exactly what will happen next.

Some of the most successful business and political leaders have true sex appeal, don't they? Let's forget about the ones who take this stuff far too literally! There is a certain charisma they exude, which is one of the highest forms of engagement. They are engaging with our desires. Imagine if you could do that with your clients; imagine if you had that kind of attraction. I want you to have that same appeal in your business dealings. I'm not saying that you will end up in bed with your clients or business partners. It's just helpful to think of the relationship and how you would like it to be, ideally. Simply by focusing on it and making an extra effort, you can control and affect people's reactions.

How to Achieve a Special Relationship with Your Customer

Make it easy for people to reach you. Be accessible. Gone are the days of the strict hierarchical organization where employees and customers had to know their place and the managing director sat in a protected ivory tower, never seen or heard from. Now, top leaders are coming into the public eye and interacting directly with customers.

The most dramatic example of this occurred in 2008 with Barack Obama's presidential campaign. To my knowledge, Obama was the first presidential candidate in history to plan and execute an entire web-based communications strategy involving email, video and blogging, and involving a growing community of supporters. The people on the Obama list received emails and links from Obama himself, as well as from his wife Michelle, publicist David Axelrod, campaign manager David Plouffe and several others involved in the campaign. The emails always came into the Inbox showing the name of the sender, exactly like any others. So, looking down your list of new messages, you would see 'Jack Smith, Michelle Obama, Mary Brown, Barack Obama...'

Just like that, they became friends and, interestingly, they always signed their communications with simply a first name, just like a friend would. Using a new medium which people responded to, the Obama campaign team ingratiated themselves easily and effortlessly into the personal networks of millions of voters. I joined the list quite late in the game, primarily for professional reasons, so I didn't see the earlier messages. All I can say is that the latter ones really built rapport with the reader and gave me the knowledge well before the election that this strategy would give them a huge lead over the other team.

Email makes it so easy to communicate with your market. However, what most companies do is send out emails from the company, which is too impersonal. People want to hear from real people and when they get emails from top people in the company, it makes them feel like they are being invited into a secret society or private club. I love getting emails from the MD or CEO of the organizations that I support, even if I suspect that person didn't actually write the email. It has his or her name and photo, and it represents the executive's personal view. The fact that the message comes from the leader gives me greater confidence in that person *and* the company, and makes me more likely to want to interact with them. That is what the Obama team did so well, growing their list to over five million people, all interested in having a dialogue with the top people.

Blogging

I hope that after the last chapter you are feeling inspired to write your blog and reach a large number of people with it. Now imagine if you focused on how you want to engage with your readers *before* you write it. A good blog is exactly like a professional journal entry. It allows the reader an insight into your thoughts and feelings, a more personal view of the company. It also allows the reader to feel they are part of a private conversation with you, which is pretty impressive considering it is a one-way medium and it may be going out to thousands of readers.

My personal belief is that executives and business owners should write their own blogs. I know there are 'ghost-bloggers' out there, and some of them are very good. One of my top contacts writes blogs for some very influential executives and he prides himself in 'getting into the executive's own voice'. But people always get upset when they find out that the blog has been written by someone else. This seems to be a greater offense even than a ghost-written book, probably because the blog is so personal.

How Personal and Vulnerable should You be?

There are some risks associated with sharing personal

information and views, as we have mentioned, but these are usually far outweighed by the opportunities presented by being vulnerable. When you are seen as a real person, you are given the benefit of the doubt and even defended when you make mistakes. Someone who shared a very private thought recently was Google co-founder Sergey Brin. In September 2008, in his public blog, Brin discussed his family history of Parkinson's Disease and his concern that he believed he was predisposed to suffer from it later in life. He wrote about the issues in a reasonable and scientific way, like the scientist he is. In my opinion, he could have gone even further, been even more personal. Despite various commentaries in the news (including my own) after the blog went live, there are currently no comments showing on the blog, so people either did not feel motivated to add their own thoughts, or perhaps comments have been deleted. But it is actually the potential of this communication that I wanted to bring to your attention. The power of sharing your real thoughts and feelings is immense, even if you can never control other people's reactions, or lack thereof.

Another legendary leader who blogs frequently and from the heart is Bill Marriott, chairman and CEO of the international hotel group. He can always be relied upon to offer solid wisdom and opinions on the state of the hospitality industry, as well as news that affects Marriott International and its customers. After the bombing of the Marriott hotel in Islamabad in September 2008, Marriott wrote in very emotional language of his distress and sadness for the guests and employees affected. Other posts are similarly open and caring, showing the real person behind the large company. In a time when companies cannot afford to be impersonal,

Marriott takes this seriously and shares more of himself than the average CEO in his industry, and indeed in many industries. In my opinion, this philosophy of involvement, visibility and trust from the head of the organization keeps the company at the top of its sector.

Be Visible

"Hello! I'm over here!"

Ivan Misner, the founder of networking company BNI, says you need to go through three stages to profitability. Firstly you need Visibility. People need to see you around and in the right meetings. Once they start seeing you, they pay attention to what you have to offer. The second stage is Credibility. We will be looking at this in a lot more depth over the next few chapters but, for a simple example, just think of someone who is not credible. Will your business relationship with them be progressing? Probably not. On the other hand, when you gain credibility in someone's eyes, you are able to achieve the third and final outcome: Profitability.

How visible are you to your customers? If you run a multinational company, it is difficult to meet people in person but, as we said earlier, video and blogging are very valuable resources today. In addition to extending your reach, videos and blogs can also be a clever means of improving engagement with new and existing clients and other stakeholders.

This is Non-negotiable

Do not make the mistake that so many business leaders make when they abdicate responsibility for client relationships. It's great to have a customer service team, highly-trained account managers and good processes. However, there is no substitute for a real interaction between the head of the business and his customers or clients. Your clients need and want to hear from you directly. Yes, it will take up some of your time, but the payback in terms of client loyalty and increased revenues will make the effort well worth it.

How to Improve Engagement

Market Research

Do you know what your market thinks of you, specifically your ability to engage and build trust and credibility? If you don't have a handle on this, nothing else you do is going to work as well as it could. It is not expensive to gather market intelligence from existing customers or even from the wider market.   You can start out by asking people what they think of you. This can be done in the form of a survey or questionnaire, or ideally in face-to-face sessions. If you suspect that your customers would give more honest answers to a third party, work with a market research company or use blind or anonymous surveys.

Who Cares? Who Cares Wins

Get out of your head and into your heart. The customers of today are tired of the information overload we talked about earlier. They need something more profound and more important, and they expect more than just superior knowledge. They expect you to care. There's a well-worn expression that is still worth repeating here: 'People won't care how much you know until they know how much you care.' It sounds so trite, but it is still true. If it sounds like fluffy stuff that has no place in the boardroom, think again. I can assure you that it is the caring organizations and especially the caring leaders who will be gaining the competitive advantage in this new business climate.

And I am talking about real caring, not pretending you care. It has to be authentic because your customers will be able to tell if you are not sincere.

I have seen so many speakers who say the right things but they just don't come across as real. For politicians, this can be deadly since people really do vote with their feet. In mid-2009, trust in certain UK Members of Parliament was eroded as a result of controversial expense claims, costing them their jobs and nearly throwing the entire system into chaos. The issue of trust is such an important one, yet trust cannot be measured scientifically. It is a feeling you only get when someone else is giving you good enough reasons to trust them. If you speak in public, pay more attention to the amount you care about your audience than the amount of information in your presentation. In my work, I see a lot of speakers present and this one key area has more influence on their success than anything else.

"If we want to be compassionate we must be conscious of the words we use. We must both speak and listen from the heart." - Marshall B. Rosenberg

The best speakers find a way to come from the heart but, sadly, some people don't know they need to do it, don't know how to do it, or don't feel like doing it. There is even one aspiring speaker I know who talks about matters of the heart and yet my own heart tells me he is a fraud. I cringe every time I hear him speak, partly because I want him to do well but partly out of embarrassment for him. I can't believe he can lie to his audiences in this way and I can't believe he doesn't see that he is deceiving them. Please don't do this. Find a way to get authentic so that you can reach people at this important level.

So, do you care about your clients? How do you know? How do *they* know? If they were asked what their heart or their gut was telling them about you, what would they say?

Those who nourish flourish.

Those who nourish flourish. It definitely pays to take care of others and make them look good. This starts with yourself and your family, then extends to your staff, suppliers and customers and, if you get really good at it, you find yourself wanting to take care of strangers. Why did Bill Gates of Microsoft set up the Bill and Melinda Gates Foundation and put so much time, effort and money into helping people in the third world? Because Bill has already taken care of himself and his family, then his employees (who apparently are among the happiest and most fulfilled in the high-tech sector), and now he feels a calling to share his success on a global basis. The authentic nature of the Gates' giving caused multi-billionaire Warren Buffett to feel compelled to share in the vision and contribute $31 billion to the charity.

"There is a loftier ambition than merely to stand high in the world. It is to stoop down and lift mankind a little higher." - Henry Van Dyke

It is my belief that when you give from the heart, it really does come back to you. This philosophy is given lip service by many leaders, but they do not follow through with positive action in every case. And we are not only talking about giving money. There is your time and attention. There is giving your opinion with the intention of helping, as we will discuss in greater detail in the next chapter. And there is the all-important leadership quality of giving others a chance to grow and contribute.

Why Start at Home?

It's common knowledge that the more successful we get, the harder it can be to take care of ourselves properly. A diet of travel, business dinners, networking, long days and heavy correspondence can leave little time and energy for exercise or careful planning of meals, much less true relaxation. But don't we all know the toll that the stress and hectic lifestyle takes after a while? We know at a rational level that we *should* take better care of ourselves, but we don't always find a way to do it.

I'd like you to think of this nurturing in a different way. I'd like you to think of the direct link between taking care of yourself and success in your business and personal life.

A client of mine told me that he had stopped drinking alcohol and now benefits from a tremendous sense of energy and clarity of thought. Other colleagues have limited their intake of refined sugars, caffeine, wheat and food additives in an effort to live a healthier life, feel better and achieve more. This is not a book on healthy living, but I had to bring this up to make my point. If you nourish yourself well, then you will have much more to give to your job and to the other important people in your life.

What do you need to do right now to feel better and to be able to give more to your work and other people in your life?

Of course, I am not just talking about nourishing yourself literally. Great leaders also find the best way to nourish their minds, their feelings and their sense of purpose. They read good quality, stimulating books. They watch programs and listen to material that makes them think. They find time to meditate, pray or simply rest. All of this makes them more able to share ideas with others in a positive way.

Engaging with the Right Media, at the Right Time

Your chosen market sector, geography, demographics etc. will all play a role in determining what type of engagement is appropriate. For example, people in their 20s and 30s are much more likely to respond to email, SMS and instant messaging than they are to face-to-face communications or direct mail arriving in the post. They also like video more than other generations do, so a marketing campaign to that age group absolutely must contain elements of video.

More Frequent Contact

If you currently speak to your clients once a year, can you bump that up to twice a year? Or even once a quarter? The number of touch points correlates directly to the overall quality of the relationship. You use alternative media so that you can 'touch' them more often.

Focus

There is a universal law that states that what we focus on improves. Simply putting some time and attention into your Engagement strategy will pay tremendous dividends. Many people probably have never had an engagement strategy and that is totally understandable. But the best leaders, the REAL thought leaders, almost certainly do. Now you have another strand that you can add to your own plan to be successful in your field. You can set yourself apart from others simply by spending time in this area because I can assure you that most people are not doing it. Being clear about your intention and doing these things – consciously at first and unconsciously later – will allow you to achieve the right level of engagement with your clients which will, in turn, create more wealth for both parties.

Chapter 6
Be a Shining Authority

When some people open their mouths, there is no doubt that they are the experts, they know what they are talking about. It doesn't matter what the subject or how many figures they throw at you, there is a sense of certainty and authority about them. This is the goal.

There is a certain assumption in our society that you need to go through various stages of learning to gather information, which can lead to knowledge and then wisdom. There are even theories on the number of hours of training and experience required to become a true expert. I would like you to suspend your disbelief for a moment and trust that there are ways of getting to 'wisdom' that don't involve putting in a requisite number of hours or steps.

Think about someone you trust for advice and guidance. It might be on a personal issue, such as health or nutrition, or it might be someone who advises you on business, financial or other matters. If you are like most people, you did not stop and count the exact number of qualifications and hours of experience they had before engaging them to help you.

Do you need followers to be leader? Some say yes; some say no. Do you need followers to be a REAL thought leader? Absolutely. Without followers, you cannot achieve any of the outcomes in our definition and make a big difference in society.

Authority comes from many sources. Knowledge and skills certainly give you a good foundation and establish you as an authority, but I'm sure you would agree that there are many knowledgeable and skilful experts out there who would never qualify as thought leaders. Equally, experience can be very valuable and can give people a position of authority.

In ten to fifteen words, describe where your experience and knowledge lie. It doesn't have to be clever; it just has to be descriptive.

_____

_____

_____

Whatever you have just written down is perfect for now.

This is the starting point. Whatever you have written down is where you start.

How can you make this statement more descriptive of your experience and knowledge? In particular, what references do you have from your experience that prove you're an expert in this area? Jot down a couple of references, examples of client work or cases studies that, if you were in a courtroom, would prove you could claim this expertise for yourself. Jot down the first things that come to mind.

_____

_____

_____

One quality that creates authority but is severely underrated is OPINIONS! As I said earlier, people have an inbuilt reluctance to share their opinions if they are worrying about others' reactions. We have also been taught to be nice and courteous to others, and the British culture is particularly keen on manners. We are our own worst enemies sometimes. Trying to be politically correct, we tone down things that we would like to say.

Your knowledge and experience give you a certain perspective. They give you an ability to decide what you think and believe about key issues in your market or in your sector, in that space that you claim for yourself. You have the ability to make statements – bold, opinionated statements – that are sorely lacking.

Remember Henry Ford? He created the production line because he believed so strongly that cars should not be produced one at a time, that there had to be a better way. Most people thought he was crazy in the early days. Henry Ford was a thought leader even when he was going against conventional wisdom, and eventually he was recognized as one of the top thought leaders of his time – maybe even of all time.

Ironically, not a hundred years later, Michael Dell took the personal computer off the standard production line because he believed so strongly that PCs should be custom-made to individual customers' requirements. Most people thought Michael Dell was crazy too, until one day they realized that Dell Computers had revolutionized that part of the industry.

These guys are real thought leaders. We know what they thought and what they believed. And we can say the same for all of the obvious thought leaders who spring to mind when we think of innovation: Jack Welch, Sir Richard Branson, Dame Anita Roddick, Dr Martin Luther King, Jr. and other leading lights.

You Have to Know What You Think

Do you know what your core beliefs are about your business, key issues in society and in your market? I have found this is the best place to start. We all know people who are serious experts in their fields. They know more than everyone else; they may be considered to be geeks. But they are rarely the real thought leaders to whom people turn when things aren't going well and new ideas are needed.

Then you Have to Know How to Put Your Points Across

In the previous chapter we discussed the importance of defining your audience. Once you have a good handle on the profile of your customers or market, you will be able to deliver your message in the right way for them. This involves getting at least five other things right:

Right length

Right medium

Right tone

Right content

Right format

Be Bold

Boldness is not a common trait. That is why it stands out. Look at the bold headings in this chapter. If the entire text were in bold, you would not be able to focus on any particular words. The reason why you want to be bold is to stand out in a crowd.

Deciding to be bold is the first step. It is a mindset. Knowing what being bold feels like is the second step. You want to be clear about what characteristics boldness entails for you (since everyone has a different way and style of manifesting their boldness). I have found that the most effective way of getting to this answer lies in the following question:

What is Not Happening in Your Life because You Have Not Been Bold Enough?

Boldness requires a good dose of emotion to come out. That emotion can be excitement, optimism, anxiety, frustration or even full-blown anger. Actually, anger is generally a good catalyst when used properly. So ironically, the youth who seem to have less respect than in previous generations may, in fact, have a greater capacity to be bold, once they learn how to temper their anger.

Polarize People; get them to Love You or Hate You

Vanilla is a good flavor for ice cream, but not for your communications. If I asked you to name a real leader, past or present, I'm willing to bet that they stand out in your mind because you love what they stand for. Equally, there may be people with whom you violently disagree on the subject matter, but you would still concede that they make a valid point, and you understand what their perspective is, even if you do not share it. The reason why you even listen to them is because they have earned your respect through a conscious or unconscious engagement strategy, as discussed in the last chapter.

> Vanilla is a good flavor for ice cream, but not for your communications.

How bold would you be, given the chance? Well, I'm giving you the chance. Your market is giving you the chance. Are you taking it?

Now is not the time to be British. As I mentioned, I have lived in the United Kingdom for nearly twenty years, so I've earned the right to say that. And I've found myself, an honorary Brit, softening things I've wanted to say, being far from bold on occasions. This is not a way to bring new ideas into the market. This is not a way to become a REAL thought leader.

Think back to those people who have created paradigm shifts with their ideas. They had to be bold and go against the grain at times. Leadership is not a job for the faint-hearted; thought leadership even less so.

People are looking for bold leadership, real thought leadership in society. No point having more vanilla; we have enough of that and it's certainly not what's needed in tough times.

Precision is Power

You also need to be precise. When we are more precise, we can create more powerful and compelling reasons for people to deal with us. Most people do not have the time or patience to figure out what value we bring to the table. We need to do that for them, being clear about what we have to say, what we think and what we want to achieve.

"Just as our eyes need light in order to see, our minds need ideas in order to conceive." - Napoleon Hill

Do you like high-level, woolly, vanilla messages? I don't, and recent surveys show that readers and customers don't, especially the younger generation.

So, if you forgot or didn't want to put your boldest, most precise, most opinionated examples in your statement above, you can add them now.

What's wrong in your industry? What are other leaders saying and doing that you violently disagree with? And why?

What truths do your stakeholders need to hear from you that no one else can tell them?

If you were to really go out on a limb, what would you say?

What do you know is true about your topic that other people need to know?

Here is some space to jot down your thoughts, if you like doing that sort of thing. If you don't like doing it, then don't.

_____

_____

_____

_____

> Most people do not have the time or
> patience to figure out what value we bring
> to the table.

Create Debate

Debate should be healthy and it should stimulate good thinking processes among thought leaders. The real reason why political debates are so important is not so that the candidates can influence each other or even the audience (it has been proven that people watch the debate already convinced about the candidates and their politics); rather it is to show the politicians' ability to think through the issues and put across their views effectively and eloquently. Unfortunately, debate has been misinterpreted by many as arguing or fighting and it is not taught in schools the way it used to be. I think if people learned how to think through their ideas and put together reasoned arguments, we would see a lot more progress on key issues.

My father used to teach speech and debate and he ran the debating club at the high school where he worked. In the 1960s and 1970s when he was in charge, I met hundreds of high school students who were invited to our house, performed in the school productions, played football or just stopped to talk to my parents when we were out shopping. My recollection is one of articulate young adults, polite and capable of having long and involved conversations with an older generation, making their points clearly and sometimes quite forcefully.

People are not learning and practising this skill, with dire consequences in society. It is an art that I do not see practised very much today and I am worried about the next generation's ability to have decent discussions and solve the major challenges we face.

I tried to encourage my daughter to join the debating club at her school and we agreed that she would wait until Year 9 because, in previous years, older pupils monopolized the club and there wasn't a good system or any training in place to help the younger pupils get up to speed. So, on the first day of term, I asked her if she was going to join the club and she informed me that it had disbanded due to lack of interest. Lack of interest! It surprises me because teenagers are so good at arguing. You'd think they would want to improve their skill level, but I guess they don't see the value.

There is a Place for Political Correctness – and it's Not Here!

Political correctness has come about because certain minority groups suffer from discrimination and perceive that it is exacerbated by tone and choice of words. I myself cringe when I read things written many years ago that refer to 'men', 'businessmen' and 'chairmen'. That kind of wording was appropriate when men dominated the workplace and made most of the important decisions in the home and in society. So it is only natural that our language should evolve to reflect the changing needs of new generations. And it is right to make every attempt to avoid offending the people with whom you communicate and the audience you want to influence. But the pendulum seems to have swung too far. When people are afraid to state what they think and feel because of concerns they will offend some individual or group, they hold back. They don't enter into discussions, challenge current thinking or propose radical changes.

The only instance where I approve of political correctness is if it is being used to avoid discrimination. Rudeness, racial slurs and insulting language are never acceptable, either in business or in personal dealings. People who stoop to that level show me that they do not value the other members of the club, or employees or whatever. And when people do not value others, they are not practising Engagement as described in the last chapter; therefore their chance of being seen as a REAL thought leader drops right down in my book.

What we are looking for is a good balance between common sense and sharing exciting new ideas.

The Blog may be the Key to a New World

Luckily the advent of the blog has loosened people's tongues and given British people instant access to a large number of outspoken individuals from different cultures. In my opinion, blogging is one of the major transformational inventions of the 21st century because of its potential to broadcast people's real thoughts, ideas and beliefs. The number of blogs and the sheer variety of topics on which people are blogging proves that we have a desperate need to tell people what we are thinking, feeling and doing.

What to Blog

If you are a business professional and you are blogging, you absolutely must think about what you are telling people. Everything you put on the internet can and will be Googled at some point. Many people use their blog to share everything that occurs to them, without much editing for appropriateness, and without much thought about the implications. Some blogs are simply 'what's going on in my world now' and REAL thought leaders ensure that it always fits within the content that they have planned.

Did I just use the word 'plan' with respect to a blog? I did. There are people who believe that blogs should be spontaneous and that planning would ruin that spontaneity. I believe in having a balance. For the past five years, I have been advising clients to use blogging as part of their overall writing and publishing strategy. You can have a thought leadership strategy and plan which includes the broad areas within which you want to influence your market. Then, every time you want to blog, you simply look for ways to tie your new entry into the strategic plan, to make sure it supports your overall message and reinforces what you have said before.

You just need to run new ideas through the filter. Most people do not have a filter, but real thought leaders know that is the only way to decide what goes in and what stays out. One of the best filtering questions you can ask is "Does this support my core message?" And another great one that I got from fellow professional speaker Molly Harvey is "Does this message or content take me closer or further away from where I want to be?"

How to Blog

There are many schools of thought on how to create your blog entries. I am not an expert on blogging; for the best advice, I unreservedly refer you to Graham Jones, based in the UK and advising bloggers worldwide. What I have learned from Graham's talks, website and private chats is that you should have an overall plan, and you should prepare some content that you want to deliver over the next few months. Go out as far as twelve months if you can. Obviously you cannot predict all of the major events that could take place over that time, but your concepts and your ideas will most likely remain stable. Put some thought into manageable chunks of information which can be read in a couple of minutes. It is better to blog little and often rather than a lot but more infrequently.

How Often?

There is no right or wrong when it comes to frequency. I believe that you should blog at the rate your readers are willing to read your updates. As you probably have no way of knowing that, you need to guess and take advice. Graham Jones suggests you blog at least once or twice a week. The added benefit is that your blog will be more likely to be picked up by the search engines that are always looking for new and fresh content.

The Value of a Good Blog

Although your blog is primarily a tool to share ideas and information, more and more business leaders are using it as their primary website. As such, you need to consider what return you will get on your blogging. It is possible to make sales on a blog site.

Seth Godin signed up 300 people within a few hours to his London-based seminar with just one blog entry. These were loyal readers of his blog, waiting for the next thing he had to say, and wouldn't you know, it was an invitation to his event!

Risks Associated with Blogging

As I mentioned above, the key is to ensure that it is part of the strategy and not some spontaneous or impulsive communication that dilutes or, worse, detracts from the carefully-planned communication to your market. You want your personality to come out because the best blogs are very friendly and conversational. This style can be over-used and overdone, and I certainly do not recommend rudeness, antagonistic behavior or lack of respect. I have personally boycotted forums and blog sites which are used as a rant and show obvious disrespect for others. Yes, the writers of the blogs may have been voicing their opinions and, as we said earlier, that is generally a good thing. However, the blog is your online presence and these outspoken individuals should have thought a bit harder before venting their spleen into cyberspace. In one case, I would have been a prospective client for the author of a particular blog. I watched and read with increasing disgust and annoyance as he tore another business person apart online.

It only took a few minutes of reading to decide that I couldn't work with someone who treated others in that way. I am so thankful, by the way, that he showed his true colors and convinced me that business relationship would *never* happen. The business was worth about $12,000, by the way. Costly error, very costly.

Speak Up with Respect and Go Against the Grain if Necessary

So what is the right tone? In June 2008, Glasgow Labour MP Tom Harris wrote a blog challenging the proponents of doom and gloom and questioning why people in British society seemed so 'miserable' when they had it so good in material terms. His comments were immediately seized upon by the media and nearly one hundred comments from readers of the blog over a two-day period.

Leaving the content of the blog to one side, which is excruciatingly hard for me as it is one of the topics that interests me more than most, we only need to observe the speed with which the MP's opponents raced to the front line to attack him and his views. There were about fifty critical responses, and then the first reader to post a comment in support of Mr Harris was Peter Morpuss, a Czech immigrant who has lived in the UK for fifteen years.

Mr Morpuss said, "I don't think you should apologise for your comments, you are honest enough to say it as it is. Too many people these days are frightened of not being PC and the result is that nothing of substance is ever said. So good on you and keep saying what you think." As soon as I add Peter to my payroll, I shall be sending him out to spread my own message far and wide.

"You may not like what I have to say..."

"Don't be afraid of opposition. Remember, a kite rises against – not with – the wind." - Hamilton Mabie

Let's take a closer look at some of the most well-known outspoken change agents in recent years: Gandhi, Mandela, Dr. Martin Luther King, Jr.. Each of these men had several gifts, only one of which was eloquent clarity. That clarity of message, however, is what stands out the most when we think of each of them. Even when they were not speaking or writing, their presence was the medium for the message. As Gandhi said, "Be the change you wish to see in the world." It's all about the message.

Do you remember when Al Gore's *An Inconvenient Truth* first hit the screens? It was as if someone had unveiled a completely new reality and I believe it was a major catalyst in government and society's recent shift in consciousness regarding our environment. Before then, Kyoto meetings and environmental policy seemed to be just rhetoric and didn't affect the lives of regular people. Now, in my own circle of friends, neighbors and colleagues, I have noticed a greater interest in finding out more about the issue, acting in a responsible way and striving to make a difference to the environment (which had not previously entered their minds).

Interestingly, the early support for Gore's message created a backlash of opposition which continues today as the environment debate rages on. However, no one could argue with the impact of this two-hour film. That's the power of clear and articulate, passionate conviction.

Where are the Women Leaders?

As I planned and wrote the above paragraphs, I had a pang of sorrow that there were no women on my list. I even thought briefly about searching my mental archives to come up with one, but the fact of the matter is that the first examples to enter my mind were all men. I have tested this idea with other people, male and female, and both groups agree that there are just not as many obvious female leaders, much less thought leaders.

There is something to be said for the fact that women to date have had an even greater challenge than men to get their views heard and noticed. And this is despite our supposed excellent communication skills. It is not a communication issue, but rather a conviction issue and, in my view, men still have the upper hand on that one. Men tend to be more confident about their views and they are trained from a young age to be strong and bold. Standing up for oneself and one's views is not always part of a woman's training, and I cannot even begin to comment on any possible genetic differences.

We are starting to see more women standing out in the political arena as well as in business. As the gender balance continues to shift, more and more women are likely to rise to the forefront, taking on roles of true leadership. The full exploration of the gender issues in communication is not within the scope of this book. However, I do have a mission to discover more female thought leaders and get them to voice their opinions boldly and widely. As such, I am doing a lot of speaking around this topic and plenty of writing.

Don't Worry, you Won't Get Sued unless you Make it Personal

As we have just seen, people are desperate for your views and if you are not sharing them, you are denying them the fullness and richness of your wisdom. If what you have to say goes against the grain, you will be in good company because every leader who has ever created important shifts in society has taken people from conventional thinking into new areas.

Unfortunately, we live in an increasingly litigious society where people are quick to blame and take others to court. So it would be reasonable for you to be wary of offending other thought leaders and going against their published opinion. However, in the free world, as long as you do not make it personal and slander individuals, you are not going to get sued for having a different opinion. It is only when you are derogatory about someone openly in writing or speech that you risk legal action. Keep the discussion to the ideas in question and not the person stating them. Check with your lawyer if it makes you feel better. I just don't want fear of litigation to stop you from saying what you think.

> People are desperate for your views and if you are not sharing them, you are denying them the fullness and richness of your wisdom.

There isn't Only Room for One Leader or Expert

There is a very strange perception in society that the market only has room for a few leaders or experts. It is based on the same scarcity mentality that stops people from sharing their best ideas. If you have ever thought 'that book's been written already', 'he or she is the guru in that area' or 'you have to be number one', then you have fallen prey to the limited thinking that there is only space for a small number of select individuals; and the corollary to that: if you cannot be number one, then you can't be a leader. Very dangerous and detrimental thinking.

Let's prove this right now. How many weight-loss books are out there in the market? Quite a few, would you agree? Are there still going to be more and more of these books published in the future? Of course. And the reason is that people are searching for answers. Do you have any leadership books on your shelf? Yes? Will you be buying any new ones that come out over the next few years? Probably. We may have ten similar books on our shelf but we will still buy the next one because we think it may contain that one distinction, one nugget or gem that will make all the difference. The author may have a new take on the subject, a slightly different angle or even one turn of phrase that resonates with the reader in a way that none of the others were able to do. People will always be searching for answers. If all the other books have not solved the problem, they will keep reading.

I've done this and so have hundreds of my friends and contacts that I've polled over the past few years. Maybe you have too. We can't all be exceptions. People will buy more than one book and listen to more than one speaker on a topic, and still get those gems that they are looking for; they will find those nuances that make it special. And as my friend Dan Poynter says, "Buying a few books is still cheaper than learning by making mistakes!"

Despite what I've just said, Differentiation is Not the Goal!

You would think twenty-plus years of marketing experience would make me a fanatic of differentiation. I do believe that in order to choose one product, service, political leader etc. over another, we need to be able to discern higher value in one than the others.

"Remember always that you have not only the right to be an individual; you have an obligation to be one. You cannot make any useful contribution in life unless you do this." - Eleanor Roosevelt

Customers use judgment and emotion to make their decisions. Remember what we said about true engagement needing to be authentic? We make decisions emotionally and then use logic to justify them to ourselves. And the greater the decision, e.g. elections, large financial purchases, major career moves, the more we use our gut feeling.

About fifteen years ago, I had to make a choice between two jobs. Both were excellent opportunities but very different. One involved managing staff, the other didn't. One required relocation; the other didn't. One involved more travel than the other. There were so many different factors involved that I finally sat down at my kitchen table and drew up a complete matrix. I gave all of the factors a weighting, then I took about an hour to think about each factor in the context of both job opportunities and score each opportunity on that factor. It was exhausting work. When I finished the matrix, I added up all the scores, multiplied them by the weightings and reached a total score for each opportunity. I looked at the paper for about a minute, then I crumpled it up into a ball because I didn't like the answer! In my gut, I had known all long which opportunity would win out and there was no need to pretend I was going to make a logic-based decision.

Now picture your clients, supporters, constituents at their kitchen tables. How will they make their decisions? How will they feel about you?

The Sad Myth of the USP

I hate the phrase USP. I try not to use it and I continuously tell clients and audiences to find a better way to market themselves. It stands for Unique Selling Proposition. How many things are truly 'unique'? Very few. I hear people say things like "Our USP is a superior level of service." Hello! I think a few other companies could say that as well. There are some excellent reasons to toss out the USP in favor of better strategies.

Firstly, the quest for the USP is based in ego. Even when shrouded as a company USP, it is still created by individuals (executive level or marketing team), so you would be right if you guessed there are always personal biases inherent in any statement of this nature. Looking for the ways in which you are cheaper, faster, more experienced, more successful or simply better than the other guy also creates bad energy and negative focus. The only way to set up these kinds of comparisons is to lead with your ego, and coming from a place of ego is not usually a nice experience for the speaker or his audience.

It is all about Influence and Authenticity

Earlier I mentioned the importance of influence in leadership positions. The goal is not how different you can be, but rather how influential. When you are more influential than the next person or business, that in itself sets you apart. And when you do this in an authentic way, a way that supports your own personal values, the irony is that you will create something totally unique. You are already unique so you can just relax and concentrate on being authentic and creating a good plan to influence your market.

You can be the 'Go-to' Person

This phrase is apparently very popular in the States and growing in popularity in the United Kingdom. The first time I heard it used was about three years ago, by my good friend and client Rob Brown. Rob is a very successful speaker and author in the area of personal reputation and customer relationships. He is a master of interpersonal relationships and practises what he preaches. One of the things in which he believes very strongly is that when people have choices between you and your competition, you must become the 'go-to' professional, the one who will be top of mind to the point where the customer would not even consider talking to anyone else. Call it loyalty, call it reputation; what it really means is that you have the edge over people who are not the 'go-to guys'.

Time and time again, I have seen successful entrepreneurs use this strategy to leapfrog their way to the top much faster than would be otherwise expected. Becoming the 'go-to' person means you can skip some of the other steps because your reputation is marching ahead of you, attracting the attention and business.

When I am referred to as the 'go-to' person in my field, it sums up the whole subject for me. That is what I want, for people to come straight to me because I have what they need. No need to shop around, no need to get into lengthy and costly bidding wars. It certainly makes things a lot simpler for busy customers, sign-posting them to the one person who can and will get them the results they want.

So if you don't like the ego aspect of being the 'go-to' person, you should at least see it as an altruistic service on your part. You are saving busy people lots of valuable time sifting through the various options available to them and you are allowing them to come straight to you.

How to Become the Go-To Person

The first thing you should do is put a bookmark in this book and run to your computer to purchase *How To Build Your Reputation* by Rob Brown! There are some wonderful tips and techniques in there that can catapult you straight to the top of your field. Then come back and read about branding and PR.

Getting Your Message Out

What I'm about to say is a bit irreverent. I spent many years in marketing and yet I think people should refuse to do marketing plans until this kind of thinking has been done. Otherwise, what is the point? I know for a fact that some marketing plans have been developed and based on very weak messages or statements. You know as well as I do that the chance of those marketing plans achieving any kind of significant success is minimal.

To execute your plan without a core message that you feel completely confident about is professional suicide.

As I mentioned before, networking is a key activity to get your message into the market and supplement the written and online communications you publish. Networking with entrepreneurs, I often meet people in the very early stages of their business, sometimes in the first few months. Even without asking them, I know they are new to business because when I ask them the golden question, their answer is waaaaaaaaay too long.

"What do I do? Well..."

The golden question, of course, is 'What do you do?' It is a golden question because it comes with a golden opportunity to give a clear and visionary answer that piques someone's curiosity and makes them interested in speaking further.

By now you will appreciate that writing a book helps you extend your reach. Being the author of a book also gives you instant authority. You can even see the word 'author' inside the word 'authority'. I think Joe Vitale first pointed this out, and what a great authority he is!

Your books, ebooks, articles, blogs and talks have the potential to make you an authority. Ensure that it is the kind of authority you want to be perceived as, by writing and publishing the best material in a strategic way.

Using PR effectively

Public relations is still the best way to get news out and achieve media coverage. You can use an agency or you can do it yourself, but someone has to be constantly monitoring the relevant news and stories coming out about your topic, and feeding news and stories to the media that present you as the authority on this subject.

For top leaders, it is generally not a good use of their time to do the legwork associated with writing professional press releases, sending them out, following them up and staying on top of all the news in the industry. Furthermore, it adds a lot more to your credibility when you have a third party endorsing you and you are not contacting people yourself, 'selling yourself'.

My own personal preference is to use a good PR agency that intimately understands what you do and what your key messages are. If they have been around for a while, they also have those valuable media contacts that will listen to them when they call or email with a hot new item. Newspapers, magazines and radio stations get hundreds of emails and faxes every week, and it is hard to get noticed. If you have an inside track in the form of a personal contact, you have a definite advantage.

Some companies get their marketing department to act as the PR function and, again, it depends on the kind of relationships they have or can develop with key contacts in the media. It is a full-time job and, in my opinion, best done by the professionals.

Your Role in PR

One way or another, you need to get others talking and writing about you. I love being quoted in the print media and being interviewed on the radio. But do you know my favorite moment? It's not during the interview. It's when they say 'Apparently you are the one to speak to about this issue'. Yes, I am. I have used PR effectively over many years to complement my own efforts at getting my message across. So when I see that investment of time and money paying off, it gives me more confidence in my PR strategy. As a small business owner, I rely heavily on the agency to spread the word about me and my good work, and I do my best to brief them and provide them with the best possible content for the press releases and approaches they make on my behalf. I am so pleased with their work that I recommend clients to them all the time so they can achieve similar results. Just ask me if you want a personal introduction.

By the way, PR opportunities are all around us, but you may need to ask! Radio stations have hundreds of hours to fill every month, and magazines and newspapers have many pages to fill. They want good content from recognized authorities on various subjects, but they may need a prompt from you.

The most important thing you can do is provide your agency with clear and articulate messages on your topic. Be PR-able! Make it easy for them to talk about you and write about you. You will need to be available for comment or interview and, if things go well, you will be invited to write opinion pieces for key publications in your industry. As we said earlier, the real thought leaders are recognized by their peers and clients because they have been actively sharing their message. They are quoted widely and they are interesting and relevant. This all takes time and I like to think of it as an investment in your thought leadership bank.

"Read all about it!"

Chapter 7
Longevity Wins in the Long Run

Longevity can be summed up nicely by one question: "How long do you stay in people's minds?" How long will they remember you when you have walked out the door, when they are in their next meeting and involved in their next crisis?

It is not really something that you can control completely. For example, if a client leaves a meeting with you and immediately receives bad news or gets into a car accident, his mind is going to be on that event, not you. But when the crisis is over and it is time to consider the matter that you had been discussing, you want to be in the forefront of his mind again, in a positive way. Longevity is something that you achieve by doing the other three things properly – reach, engagement and authority. It's a bit of a windfall.

How Long will *You* be Talked About?

You will know about my good friend and client Rob Brown from the last section. Rob is a very prolific author. A few years ago, he worked with me to produce a 300-page book called *How to Build Your Reputation*, and I knew he had written a few other booklets. What I didn't realize until he showed me his impressive Educational Resources catalogue is that he now has a total of 64 different products (books, booklets, reports, CDs and much more) and he is producing more each month. So this qualifies him as an expert on the subject of getting your message out. A few months ago, we had dinner and I shared the REAL philosophy with him. He immediately gave me his viewpoint on the aspect of longevity.

What really makes you stick in someone's mind, Rob says, is Recency and Relevance. If what you have to say is relevant, people will pay attention. Well, that makes perfect sense. But, as we said, what happens when they go to the next meeting, or start wading through their next 100 emails or meetings? Despite the initial interest, your prospective clients could forget about you, so you need to keep reminding them of your key messages. They need to have heard from you, or about you, recently. You can do this in the form of emails, newsletters, blogs and seminars. All of these keep feeding your message to your clients. But what about the book you wrote last year? That can also be re-introduced in the form of new versions such as audio or electronic, as well as links, reviews, articles and interviews based on the book, and referencing the book.

I'd like to add one more 'R' to the definition of Longevity. That would be Reference – giving people something to refer back to after they leave your presence.

So you want people to remember you after they meet you. Think back to your childhood and the leaders you looked up to at that time. Now, years later, I am asking you to remember certain leaders and they are still in your mind. What was it about them that created that respect, why do they still stand out in your mind?

Printed books and other tangible products are essential for reminding people about you. Books (and remember, when I say 'books' I include books in print, ebooks, audio books and any other format) are still the main vehicle for getting your message across to your market and staying there.

No matter what else you do to boost your longevity, get into print.

They Want to Take You to Bed with Them

When speaking to leaders who do presentations, I often say that that their audience wants to take them to bed with them. It gets a good laugh, and of course it is designed to. It's true, though, isn't it? Many people like going to bed (or on the train or wherever else we like to read) and enjoying the content of a good book in peace and quiet; it might as well be your book! Sometimes people can't absorb the full impact of your speech during the forty minutes you are with them. Sometimes they want to go through your main points again, in more detail. Sometimes they just want to have a permanent reminder to hand. Think about the possibilities: they can highlight passages in the book, turn the page down, bookmark things to go back to later. As good as your speech may be, it cannot possibly do any of those things.

People want to take you home with them

However, there is a serious underlying message here. No matter how great you are on stage, no matter how interesting and compelling the conversation you have just had with them, the minute you leave other things start encroaching on their time and attention. They begin to forget about you as other things take over. It happens to all of us. The best way to avoid being forgotten is to give people plenty of things that can be 'in their face' when they go home. So far, videos are proving a popular method for learning about business topics. They may as well watch yours!

Get Others Talking and WRITING about You

You want to hear someone say "I keep reading about you everywhere" (as long as it's good publicity!). That is proof that your strategy is working. But good PR rarely comes out of the blue. It requires a strategic approach and constant high-level control and maintenance from you, the business owner.

I don't know if you use a PR agency, have PR people or a marketing team, or maybe you do it yourself. No matter which route you choose, you still need to be the one that drives the strategy. You will need to be involved in the plan to ensure that it achieves your objectives. And, most importantly, you will need to provide the content to anyone else who is writing about you and for you. Because if you don't, you risk having the message diluted, misinterpreted or even sabotaged by well-meaning efforts.

Create a Family of Messaging Materials

Another thing to remember is that you are not going to have only one thing to say in your life. I am always amazed by people who write 20, 30, 40 books in their lifetime. They are obviously very talented, but the truth is that they have also spent more time doing strategic thinking about their subject than most people in their field. Maybe not every book is a bestseller, but they certainly help create an impressive profile. Would you rather have ten good books in the market or just one? Right.

Now I'm not talking about fiction here; that's different. We probably all have an unlimited number of fictional books and stories in us that we could bring out if we had the time. I'm talking about all the key messages you could develop around your topic. If you spent enough time thinking about it and doing effective planning and strategy work, you might find that you have quite a few different yet complementary ideas that form a body of work.

You are also more than capable of producing several ebooks, series of articles, excellent blogs, keynote presentations, videos, podcasts, PR... the list is practically endless. Once you have done the planning and outlined your content, you can send that content into the market with confidence and clarity, knowing that everything is synchronized, supporting the other materials, working together to set you up as a REAL thought leader in your field.

Think of Richard Branson. How many different ideas and businesses has he had? There is an overall theme to his ventures: entrepreneurship, innovation, risk and fun. He now has several books out, and the story of his success has been written up in a couple of good biographies. He has been interviewed extensively (despite a life-long aversion to public speaking, Branson has managed to overcome it just enough to build his brand), and he uses his internal staff and external PR agency to disseminate his messages into the market exactly the way he intends.

To Write a Book or Not to Write a Book – That is the Question

We have just spent time looking at how serious thought leaders get their message out and, in most cases, a printed book is at the hub of their strategy. I have a huge bias towards writing and publishing, I recognize that. But I also recognize that not everyone wants to write a book or they feel it is not the right time for them. I get that. So, if that is you and, despite everything I have outlined, you are not keen to write and publish your book, then you can simply skip the next chapter. Seriously. There are plenty of other ways to get your message across effectively and build your reputation as a REAL thought leader in your field. A good-quality printed book is the best, easiest and quickest way to achieve it, but it is not the be-all and end-all. Go ahead and go straight to the chapter that suits you best.

Chapter 8
How to Write a Book the REAL Way

Still with us? Good. I will reward you with some excellent strategies to plan, write and deliver your book faster and better than you ever dreamed possible. Working in this field for so many years has given me insights and 'golden nuggets' that I can now share with you, to help you save many hours of hard work and struggle.

The first thing you need to understand is that thought leadership often means breaking away slightly from traditional thinking. Nowhere is this more true than in the world of publishing. With half a million books coming out each year, the publishing game has changed significantly. It is easier than ever to get a book into print, and harder than ever to sift the quality from the rubbish. The traditional publishers are changing, slowly, but they still tend to work in a specific way. Other options are available, each with their own advantages and disadvantages, so you need to get clear on what is most important to you before leaping into this area.

The Market for Your Book

Traditional book publishers invest in an author's book; therefore they want to ensure they get a good return on their investment. That's understandable. It's a business case. So how to do they know whether to invest or not? The first thing they do is look at the books people are buying and decide if there is a large enough market for your topic. They look at books that are similar to yours. If they can't categorize you, they may feel there is no market for your book.

What's all this about 'books that are similar to yours'? What's that all about? That doesn't sound like an emphasis on thought leadership. Exactly. It isn't. The moment you start comparing and finding similarities with other books, you lose the thought leadership game. Most traditional publishers want something that sounds new and innovative, but not too 'out there'.

If you want to make your mark as a REAL thought leader, you need to rely on your own instincts as well as common sense. Instead of doing massive amounts of market research to see what other people are writing about and what is selling, YOU decide what you want to say and you CREATE the market. New markets are created all the time and all it takes is a spark of inspiration, a little education and lots of perseverance.

Just because people are not buying something does not mean there is no need. It may mean that they have not yet recognized they have a need. Before mobile phones were ubiquitous, did you think that you would ever become dependent on one? If you are honest, I'll bet there was a time when you were still saying you would NEVER own a mobile phone or be a slave to one...

If you want to write and publish the book YOU want to write, then you don't really need to look to others to validate your concept. I get calls and emails on a daily basis from people who want me to tell them whether their book idea will sell. I'll tell you what I tell them: "How the heck should I know?!" Sometimes the books that we think will do very well actually bomb, and others come out of the blue to become bestsellers. Authors and publishers do their best to forecast and predict book sales, but there is no crystal ball and no real way of knowing how a book will do. A very large publisher told me that out of every ten books they publish, three lose money, five break even, and only two become big sellers. That tells me that many times even the big guys get it wrong, in fact eight times out of ten! And that is after all the careful analysis which led to those ten books beating hundreds of others that ended up in the slush pile.

Am I saying you should not think about your market or do no market research at all? Absolutely not. I am just saying that you don't want to analyze the statistics to death or put too much emphasis on them, especially if you want to write something that can't be categorized very easily.

I think it is a hundred times more important to put your thoughts down exactly as you want to, and get the book into print quickly and into the hands of people who need to hear your message. They'll tell you how well your book will do. They'll vote with their feet.

No Ghosts Allowed

At least once a week, I get a very senior business leader on the phone telling me he wants to write a book but he has no time so he needs a ghost-writer. Let me see... how can I say this nicely... no ghosts! Some of my best friends are ghost-writers and there is a time and a place to use them. There are some good ones out there who, when briefed properly, can write in another person's voice. But what most people try to do is outsource and offload the overwhelming task they have defined as their book project. They think it is a type of shortcut.

Whether the writer is named or not, passing the responsibility of putting together your ideas is usually inauthentic, ineffective, inefficient - and it's cheating. It may seem tempting to get someone in to do the writing and it may even look like it would save time, but I'm going to show you that, in most cases, it doesn't save any time and actually diminishes the effect of the book. I've lost track of the number of people who have told me they were so unhappy with the way their ghost-written book turned out that they started over and did it themselves (or came to work with me).

"No ghosts allowed!"

Real Thought Leaders Write Their Own Books

Writing a full-length book the smart way only takes between 50 and 100 hours of work, total. This can be spread over a three- to six-month timeframe or it can be done during a week or two where the desk is clear and you are not going to be interrupted. It doesn't matter which way you do it; you are still looking at a finite amount of work. I am not very impressed with so-called 'business leaders' who will not put 50 to 100 hours into what is probably the most important job they need to be doing: influencing their market.

There are ways to get the writing time a lot closer to the 50 hours than the 100 hours. If you are still reading, then I guess you have not taken offense at my last point, so I will reward you with a tried and tested methodology that has allowed hundreds of my clients to produce excellent books and articles quickly and easily.

Planning

The first key is good planning. If you want to know why most people never start, much less finish writing a book, the answer is 'planning'. Why do many books need extensive editing? Again, 'planning'. What about the ones that turn out too long, too short, disjointed, lacking the right flow, tone, style, content, illustrations, examples or descriptions? You guessed it: 'planning'. Over the past eight years of working exclusively with authors, I have gathered a lot of evidence from the stories people tell me and, in particular, the mistakes they have made when trying to write books. It almost always boils down to the lack of a good plan. It seems that there is a perception that writing is creative and needs to flow; inspiration is valued above all else and the image of a lonely writer tapping into his creative genius and typing away in isolation prevails. "Where is the plan?" you may ask and be told that they don't want to put too much structure around their book idea; they think it will kill the creativity.

Guess what? It's just the opposite! When you take the time to build an excellent plan, you actually allow your creative energy to flow more in the knowledge that it is fulfilling that plan. Business books certainly need to be planned out in minute detail. You can't risk having them turn out any other way than the way they need to be.

Your plan needs to contain much more detail than you ever thought necessary. I like clients to nail their thoughts at the planning stage and provide so much direction for the writing that the book can pretty much write itself. The process has been called 'connect the dots' but that may be a bit simplistic, implying that there is no skill involved.

Dig Deep

If you think of a standard outline, you can picture different levels. With mind-mapping, it is no different except that the levels go outwards from the center, instead of indented in a list. At the core or heart of your plan is your key message, and your sub-messages fan out from there. They all make specific points and are supported by even more detailed messages and themes, at levels three and four. Somewhere around level four or five, you need to articulate which examples you plan to use to make your points. The exact structure of your plan depends on the topic and the context, but the essential requirement is that you get very specific during the planning phase. In my experience, most authors fall down in this area because they don't get specific enough. They think they know what information will go in each section; it's in their heads. When you work with a sketchy outline, it is kind of like trying to get to your destination without having all of the roads listed on your map. If only the major roads are on the map, that will get you so far, but not to the exact destination to which you are heading.

The first problem occurs while the author is trying to get the first draft down on paper. Without a thorough plan for the content, there is not enough direction and the author can get paralyzed, thinking it is 'writer's block' when in fact it is just a lack of direction. If you have to stop and think of what to say when you are in the middle of writing because you have not planned it well enough in advance, you go into left-brain thinking immediately. This can block access to the right brain and all of its creative potential, just when you need it most!

When you move from the planning phase to the writing phase, you will soon know if your plan is good enough. The first draft you produce is simply called the 'first draft'. Some people refer to the first draft as a rough draft. I don't mind what you call it, as long as you don't use a phrase I hate: 'brain dump'. Not only is that an unpleasant image, it also implies a hugely wasteful, ineffective and messy way to get

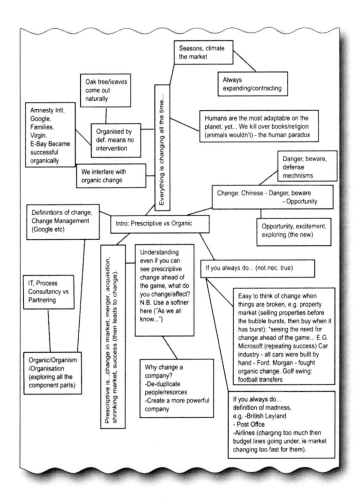

**Excerpt from Philip Cox-Hynd's plan for
Change by Choice**

your thoughts down on paper. In my experience, writers who create really messy first drafts have so much editing to do that it becomes a chore and takes far longer than it would have done otherwise. In many cases, these drafts are beyond help and never see the light of day. How sad! Be honest, do you have any articles, books or other projects that you 'drafted' out and then could not edit into something sensible?

At the other end of the spectrum is the situation where you end up with a first draft that is too short and sketchy and needs much more material. I don't call that a 'proper' first draft, more like half a draft. A few years ago, I was working with an amazing business leader who had a very clear idea for his book. Together we took his content plan to the first and second levels, and his job was to flesh it out a lot more before starting any writing. Unfortunately, we had all of our conversations by telephone after that since he was travelling, and he assured me he had completed his plan. (You know where this is heading, don't you?) Suddenly, he was finished with his first draft and it was way too short! It then needed a lot of work to add a lot of material and it was hard work.

Whatever you do, make sure you have an excellent plan for your book, one that will sustain you on your writing journey and give you the results you want. One of the best plans I ever saw was that of John Caines, a client who worked with me in 2006 and wrote *The Effective Entrepreneur*. John is a seasoned business expert and consultant with much experience to share. He was at risk of trying to put everything he knew about business into the book and it certainly would have turned out too long. Instead, John followed The Book

Midwife® methodology and he created a structure for his content that went five levels deep in most cases, with even more detail in others. Every example, anecdote, question

			(cedure later)	
[THE BIG] KEY IDEAS	Goal Setting. Delegating and monitoring	Goal	Self	
			Task	
			Team	
		Delegate	Rapport	
			Resources	
			Feedback confirmation	
		Monitor	Intervals	
			Tolerances	
			Intervention	
		Achievement	Know when you've succeeded	
			Feedback [quickly]	
			Celebrate [quickly]	
	Pace Making		MIS team	
			Elastic band analogy	
	Why am I doing this (inner game)	Not just 'economic man'	Maximising expected value	
			Maximising possible value but with high risk – or breaking moral code	
			A score sheet	
		Business frame	Definition of business success?	
		Whole life frame	Other parties	
THE END GAME	Your Business	Indefinite life or project ?for		

Excerpt from John Caines' plan for
The Effective Entrepreneur

and exercise was planned well before he did any writing, which allowed him to go into depth on those ideas without getting distracted or ending up on a tangent. What resulted was a wonderfully engaging, thorough and sensible book on effective leadership, one that he has used with hundreds of clients and conference delegates.

Write your First Draft Quickly

Do you know, most people never even finish writing a first draft of their book? If you get to that point, you will be ahead of 95% of the population. The easiest way to get your draft down on paper is to follow your carefully prepared plan (assuming you took my advice above). You can take your full outline and put it into a program like Microsoft Word. Then go through it, point by point, fleshing out all of the items you listed. This is, in fact, how I am typing this manuscript right now. The most important thing is to write it fast. With a good outline, there is no such thing as writing it too fast, and you will not risk having it end up too long, too short or off-track.

Don't Try to Make it Perfect

So many people want their books to be perfect, and I don't blame them. However, the first draft stage is not the time to be worrying about perfection. If you find yourself going through what you have written over and over again, you are being too nit-picky. You may be avoiding moving it forward, which in some cases can indicate a fear of success, disguised as fear of failure. You are also putting yourself into that left-brain logical, analytical mode which, as I said, is definitely not helpful for creating new material.

A good way to deal with the temptation to edit is to highlight the bit you want to go back to in the online document, so that you can always find that bit and edit it later. One client of mine cleverly used double asterisks (**) to mark the places he wanted to return to. Then he could find all of those instances of double asterisks when going through the first draft, so he didn't miss any. You wouldn't want your book going to print with "**needs more here" in it, would you?! Unfortunately I have seen this happen – not with my clients' books, I hasten to add!

Editing your Manuscript

Editing is a tricky subject. The main reason is that it is completely subjective and there is no way of getting around that. It is also a very big area and encompasses two very different processes. If we break the subject into the two discrete processes, it will be easier for you to understand.

Content and Context Editing

If you have completed a first draft of a full-length book, then I commend you! Only about five percent of all people who intend to write a book even get to finished first draft stage. The first thing you need to do (after patting yourself on the back) is to go through the entire manuscript as objectively as you can, doing a complete self-edit. This is challenging but essential, since you want it to be in the best possible shape before you start sharing it with others.

Look for completeness, duplication, inconsistencies and accuracy. Look for sections that you meant to research but forgot. Try to look at it as though it is someone else's work. The best way to do this is to use a printed version and go through it with a red pen, just like your teacher used to! Mark it all up and then make the changes you identified.

The next thing you need to do is to get some of your trusted colleagues or peers to take a look at your manuscript. If you haven't used a book coach, it's most likely you will have been working in complete isolation and not had any feedback. This is a chance to test your material with people you can trust, and you may get some very valuable comments from them which you can use to improve your book.

Over the years, I have developed a fool-proof system for getting good quality feedback in a timely manner. First, you need to have identified your peer reviewers at an early stage and gained their agreement to look at your manuscript. There are several reasons why they would be willing to help you: for example, they might do it just because they know you and like you; they might owe you a favor or they might want to get something in return, even if it's just a dinner or being mentioned in the acknowledgements section of your book.

Second, you will only give them a short time to review the

document. The reason for this is obvious when you think about it. When we have a long lead time, we sometimes put the task to the bottom of our priority list, with more urgent items taking precedence. If you give your readers exactly a week to get back to you, they will almost always do it on time. They can't afford to put it off or forget about it.

You will give them a strict set of questions to answer as they go through your material. You need to give them enough guidance but don't overwhelm them with too many questions.

Despite all this, you may find that people give you unsolicited feedback on other aspects of your book; they may give you contradictory feedback (e.g. one person loving a particular example and another hating it) or they may ask you to make changes you don't feel right about. In the end, the final decisions are yours. You are the one who has put all the time and effort into producing a full-length book. Take the advice you get and consider it carefully, but make the decisions that are right for you, your book and your market.

Bringing in the Professionals

Professional content and context editing, or developmental editing, is like a dark art. No one is able to define exactly how it works, except to acknowledge that when the editor does a good job, the manuscript is neat, tidy, of the right length and sounds more like the author than the original version! I have the highest respect for this kind of editor and I only work with a select few in the industry who treat the work sensitively and keep the author's 'voice' authentic.

For those business authors who believe they have great ideas but are not good writers, this may be the best option. Get the manuscript to this point with proper planning, all the right content in the right structure and, most importantly, in the executive's own style, and then get someone to give it the once-over, correcting inconsistencies, making it sound better, clearer and sometimes even more interesting. I believe there is nothing wrong with that because at least we have the concepts and ideas from the leader's head and key content and stories in his own words.

I do, however, have a big problem with people who want to write a load of garbage and then expect an editor to 'fix it'. There is absolutely no need for a major overhaul if the planning has been done properly and the book has been put together consciously adhering to the outline. One of the best compliments I ever received was from a major business publisher (Prentice Hall Life, part of Pearson) who was publishing one of my clients' books: *Change your Life with NLP* by Lindsey Agness. I bumped into the Pearson folks at London Book Fair and I asked them how Lindsey's book was coming along. When I mentioned the name of the book, the publisher smiled in recognition. "Oh, yes," he said. "I remember that one. It came to us in very good shape and needed very little editing indeed." That is a sign of a good manuscript that has been put together with care. All publishers prefer books that require minimal editing because that reduces 'slippage', a common problem in the industry that simply means the book does not hit its deadlines and sometimes impacts the launch date.

The true implication of all this is of course that you can save a lot of time, hassle and money. You can also avoid a very nasty experience – the one where your beloved manuscript comes back bleeding red ink from the many corrections and suggestions. Far too many people get disheartened when they receive a manuscript back from the editor with hundreds of changes and corrections that need to be made. Despite all the time spent so far, many give up at this point, refusing to put in the extra work that is required to fix it. The manuscript never gets published, which, I'm sure you'd agree, is a huge shame.

Line-Editing or Copy Editing

Often called 'proofreading' by people unfamiliar with the process, line editing is a cleaning and fixing process that captures spelling and punctuation errors, fixes grammatical errors and inconsistencies and gives you a very polished result. There is no excuse for putting a book, article or web content into the market with typos or errors that could have been identified and corrected. All good publishers insist on professional editing of this nature, and you, the author, need to be vigilant about quality control as well.

If you manage to get a book deal with a traditional publisher, editing is usually provided for you, but you will still need to check every page because nobody is perfect. Every day I see typographical errors in professionally published books that somehow got into print, despite rigorous controls and checks.

If you opt to self-publish your book or work with one of

the reputable cooperative publishers, you will be expected to source and fund your own editing, although they may offer you a service for a fee. Please do your homework and ensure you are using a professional, trained editor who has plenty of experience working on full-length book.

Books need a professional edit

Publishing Options for REAL Thought Leaders

It is still true that the greatest reach can be achieved by spending time, money and effort on marketing. Traditionally, the large publishers spend the most promoting books, getting them onto bookstore shelves and getting publicity for their authors. There are some drawbacks in using a traditional publisher, but their capacity is still great to reach large numbers of potential readers and sell more books. That is why it is still a popular choice.

Try to Get a Book Deal, but Don't Waste too much Time

It typically takes 12-18 months from the signing of a publishing contract to see a book in print. The exact timings depend on how much of the book is written at the time of the deal, scheduling constraints at the publisher's end, promotional and marketing activity that needs to take place before the launch and other factors.

If you add to that timeframe the amount of time you may spend finding an agent and/or a publisher, the total could run to several years or more. Indeed, I know many people who have been 'trying' to get a book published (by traditional publishers) for years. You may know some as well.

I usually advise clients to have a Plan A and a Plan B. Plan A involves finding an agent and a publisher and getting to a successful deal. If you put a time limit on this phase, then you are unlikely to let months and years go by in fruitless pursuit of your goal.

Plan B is becoming more popular, as it involves the author taking control of the process and either self-publishing or using the services of a cooperative publisher. The main difference is that there is an investment on the part of the author, whereas in the traditional publishing scenario, there is no investment payable, and sometimes the publisher even pays the author a small advance. I am not going to go into detail about the publishing industry here, but you can have a free report outlining and discussing the three main options simply by sending an email to info@bookmidwife.com with the subject 'Free publishing report please'.

Chapter 9
What Really Stops Most People from Going for BOLD

In Chapter 1 of this book, I identified a human need to strive for recognition and acknowledgement for our achievements. In order to get that recognition, we need to let the world know about our ideas and accomplishments.

What Stops People from Expressing Themselves?

For years, I have been studying the factors that stop people from expressing themselves. Although there are many, they almost always fit into the category of 'fear'. No matter how well educated we are, no matter how accomplished and experienced, we all seem to let fear rule our decision-making at one time or another. I have worked with executives of very large companies who surprised me with their hesitancy to put forward new ideas. Caution and judiciousness are very useful, but used in excess they create fearful feelings that can literally stop people from achieving greatness.

The Different Faces of Fear

"I have nothing to say"

What do you mean, you have nothing to say? Are you sure you want people to think that about you? If I may do a bit of mind-reading here, what I think people mean when they say this is that they don't have anything original to say. And this is closely related to an assumption that unless you have something super-original and never-heard-before, then it is not worth saying anything. Do I even need to point out the lunacy of this argument? Now, I admit that I prefer to read interesting articles and books with new and different viewpoints that I may not have considered before (as opposed to the same old boring, tired, clichéd drivel that has been rehashed too many times already). But I can usually find at least some new points, or even one. So many people say that if they get even one nugget from reading a book or listening to a talk, then it was worth it. One nugget? I think you are capable of delivering that.

According to Philip Cox-Hynd, a client of mine and well-respected change management consultant, the hesitation comes from a perception gap, and that gap widens in direct proportion to the seniority of the leader in question. For example, an executive who has been promoted believes that there is an even higher expectation of him than before, perhaps that he should be perfect or without fault. This causes extreme tension and agitation and makes the executive act more cautiously to avoid even the slightest risk of being 'found out'. Ironically, Philip procrastinated for many years, letting this exact fear paralyze him, before finally working with me to produce the superb leadership book *Change by Choice*.

"To be a great champion you must believe you are the best. If you're not, pretend you are." - Muhammad Ali

A few months ago, I was talking to a client who was struggling to finish her book. She is one of the top ten people in her industry, yet her book has taken 16 years to develop. She brought me in because she had two conflicting emotions about the book but the one called 'desire' finally grew stronger than the one called 'fear'. When we started looking at what was really going on, we discovered that there were some legitimate-sounding excuses for delaying the completion and launch of the book but, in reality, they were all fear-based. It seemed that the more senior and the more successful she became, the less risk she was willing to take in terms of exposing herself and her ideas to the market. You could say that she had more to lose, and some instinct in her sub-conscious was simply trying to protect her from the critics.

Oh, I nearly forgot to tell you the most interesting bit. About halfway through the conversation, she told me that she was not interested in putting the book out unless it was going to be a success. When I asked her what her definition of success was, she said it meant selling one million copies of the book. When we probed a bit more and got under the surface, it transpired that this was a convenient way to avoid publishing the book and exposing herself to her critics, because she didn't really believe she would sell a million books (and she's probably right – most people don't sell a million books). The shift happened when she agreed to redefine success as getting a book into the market to share her story.

It never ceases to amaze me how many top leaders fall into this trap. The trap of believing that the risk of exposure outweighs the opportunity to share wisdom. They pepper their correspondence and conversations with innocent enough conservative language, but that is a language I understand and can translate into straight talk. When I challenge them on it, they usually laugh and agree, and then we can get on with the task at hand. That's the great thing about true leaders: they take responsibility.

Now, in a publicly-held company, the shareholders sometimes hold the reins and the executives have to answer to them, as well as to the board, the management team, employees and customers and even, increasingly, the media. So it can seem even riskier for this type of company executive to come out with controversial ideas and opinions. And, of course, the book will need to go through various approvals, but that shouldn't stop someone from writing.

Being bold is about standing out

We hear expressions like 'Don't rock the boat' and 'Don't stick your head above the parapet'. Well, sorry but I don't believe any major breakthroughs could ever happen without at least a little boat-rocking or someone sticking their head above the parapet.

"Is my idea important enough?"

I hear this question a hundred times a week in my work. However it always surprises me when I hear it from successful business people who are achieving results in many areas of their life. There must be something so big and scary about putting your ideas into the market that it makes even the superstars quake in their boots. I completely understand the rationale. As I said earlier, we have a great need to feel important and we want our ideas to be seen as important. What we don't realize, however, is that this question can never be answered in a definite way. That is, there is no way of knowing how to rate an idea on a scale of importance, which is completely subjective anyway. If you ask me to read an article, I may like it but may not feel it is important to me. However, there could be someone next door that thinks it is the most important thing they have read all year.

When this is the primary question, the person asking it is almost always thinking that unless they get a positive answer, they will not share their idea with the world. The fear of being seen as unimportant is too great.

At the root of this are other more worrying questions: "What will people think?" "Will they like what I have to say?" "Will they like ME?"

These questions stop more potential leaders than any other questions I have ever heard. Let's tackle them one by one, or rather by two and one, since the first two go together.

"What will people think? Will they like what I have to say?" This is complete and utter abdication of our value to the whim or opinion of others. Remember what Einstein's teachers thought of him? They thought he was a dreamer and would never amount to anything. How about Gandhi? Can you imagine how the history books would read if Gandhi had worried about what people would think about his standing up to the government, going on a hunger strike or mobilizing hundreds of thousands of people without an official political role?

If you are struggling with this particular fear, you are allowing your worry about other people's opinions to overshadow all potential greatness of your best ideas.

"Will they like ME?" How often does this question show up in your life? As human beings, we do want to be liked, but if this is the driving force behind our actions, we are doomed to become less than our potential.

Many leaders do not like to admit that they care about being liked. It doesn't seem to fit with our definition of leadership and it smacks of being soft and unprofessional. However, it is a real need and we should acknowledge it, while keeping it in perspective.

Jack ran a large sales team and was constantly under pressure from his boss. He got to work early every day, switched his mobile on in case any of the sales guys needed him, and made sure he was on top of the figures and prepared. Jack's team consisted of a few overachievers and a large number of average producers. Towards the end of every month, Jack would hold more meetings and calls with his guys, the pressure intensifying with each meeting. "I don't care if they like me," Jack told me. "They respect and value my leadership." And just in case, Jack went out on a few extra calls with his guys at the end of the month, to help them close a few more deals. When questioned about the mediocre performers, he would make excuses for them and never seemed to have enough reason to let them go. I think Jack cared about being liked much more than he let on.

'Our Fearless Leader'

To enable your best leadership qualities to come out, you need to liberate yourself from the shackles of these very unhelpful questions. You may have heard the phrase 'our fearless leader'. The fact is that the person in question is not completely without fear but he/she does not let it rule their life. If you picture a great war hero such as Winston Churchill or Napoleon, it is hard to imagine them being worried about what others would think or whether people would like them. Maybe they *did* worry about things like that, but those thoughts didn't stop them doing what they needed to do.

Think about your most radical idea. Go on, think about it now. You know the one I mean. It's the idea that is so big and so exciting that when it comes into your consciousness, you shoo it away because it is a bit too scary.

Have you got it in mind? Good. Now, picture yourself telling your most important client all about it. What do you think they will say? What is the worst thing that could happen? You might think people will laugh at you, but that rarely happens. More likely, you will get arguments from cynics and sceptics who simply see your idea in a negative light or don't understand the benefits. And you simply need to arm yourself with confidence and perhaps some facts that can help them see things your way and, if not, give you the motivation to proceed regardless of what others think.

You have to find ways of dealing with your fear so it doesn't stop you from realizing your greatness. I have read lots of books on the subject, and maybe you have too. I have also discovered some techniques that really work. The most powerful thing you can do is to build up a strong picture and story of why you are right and why your idea is so good. You can completely overpower any negative thinking with positive energy that can propel you into action.

Have you ever faced one of your biggest fears? I have walked across burning coals, jumped off very high poles and made telephone calls that literally caused me to shake with fear. Funnily enough, the thought of some of the telephone calls was worse than the burning coals! Most of the fear is in the build-up phase, before the event. We can blow some things out of proportion to such an extent that they totally consume us and paralyze us. The irony, though, is that the most important achievements in our lives are usually linked to experiences where we find ways to act despite our fears. I can think of at least three examples of this in my career and after the fact, I felt an almost superhuman power, confidence and pride that I would not have felt if I had stayed on the ground or hadn't made that call. Simply proving to yourself that you can face your fears is one of the most powerful lessons we can teach our subconscious. I am not an expert in this area, nor do I want this to be a psychology book. I just want you to achieve everything that you deserve.

Other Factors that Get in the Way

Time

As you may have heard, we all have 24 hours in a day. In Chapter 2, we looked at the four quadrants where we spend our time. When we don't achieve what we set out to achieve, it is often because we make poor use of time, and we don't make enough time for the important things. When you are supposed to be working on strategic plans and critical work, do you allow unexpected events and other people to interrupt you and take you away from what you are supposed to be doing? Real thought leaders tend to use their time well and spend enough time on the important and strategic tasks, like thinking and conceptualizing.

Lack of Discipline

I spoke about being disciplined with our time but what about your thoughts and ideas? Do you allow thoughts to come into your head all the time, distracting you, taking you off course and making you doubt your current strategy? The greatest leaders allow themselves appropriate time to think and develop ideas. They also have strategies in place to follow through on ideas and think things through properly. My best clients go through the thinking process thoroughly to develop their ideas for books, articles, blogs, or whatever they need to produce. They work on the right messages at the right level and build a good level of confidence in their thinking because it has gone through a methodical process. That way, when other ideas pop into their head, or colleagues introduce concepts that contradict theirs, these thought leaders have a chance to look at the new ideas and compare them with their own robust and fully-developed ideas. At that point they can decide if they want to change anything about their original idea, but they do not get blown from one idea to the next like a rowboat on a stormy sea.

Ignorance

How many times do we listen to the advice of well-meaning friends and relatives who have no clue about our business? We go to the wrong sources for answers instead of working with the experts. We buy into the myths and the hype of the media. Our friends, relatives and even the media (or should I say, *especially* the media) are completely ignorant about out own unique perspective on things and our strategy for getting our message into the market. When it comes to building a REAL thought leadership strategy, ignorance is not bliss.

Ignorance can also show up in the form of hiding one's head in the sand like an ostrich. Earlier, I condemned those who rely too heavily on external views of the market. However, you need to have a good, realistic handle on the market you want to conquer. There is a case for good, solid market research that confirms you are at least going to have a group of people to influence!

Lack of Confidence

This surprisingly common executive ailment can stop people dead in their tracks. It is a reality but it should not be used as an excuse. It can usually be solved quite easily with appropriate training, consultancy and practice. I have lost count of the number of executives I have spoken to who say things like "I'm not a writer", "I can't write", "I'm not a good public speaker". Maybe you have even said similar things to close friends or coaches, or just thought them.

The funny thing is that when people say "I can't write", this often means they can't spell, and they are voicing a mantra which may have started many years ago with a teacher marking up their paper in red ink. I find that for so many people, that kind of experience set off a whole chain of events and beliefs that destroyed the person's confidence in his ability to get his ideas across. Spelling and grammar are easy to fix! As I mentioned before, we have spell-checking software and skilled editors and proofreaders to tidy up manuscripts. The main thing is to get your ideas down on paper and not let the criticism of some teacher thirty years ago stop you from sharing your wisdom with the world. The statements may or may not be true, but in any case they cannot be allowed to rule your life. Furthermore, there are certain tasks that executives need to carry out as part of their job description, and writing and speaking are usually up there at the top of the list.

If you do not have confidence in these areas, there is a plethora of training courses, coaching and reading material available to you, to improve your skill level. I suggest that every time a little voice pipes up and says to you "that's not one of your strengths", you should listen to it and start a list of action items to deal with it. Or stop and get things in perspective. You do not need to be good at absolutely everything, and you can get help and support on most tasks. But if you want to be an effective leader, you must be willing and able to write and speak.

Chapter 10
REAL Wealth
(Hint: it's not just about Gold)

So you have a choice to make. It is the same choice you make every day of your working life. Do you go out on a limb and put your thoughts and ideas into the world, or do you play it safe? In other words, do you fulfil your purpose and your responsibility as a leader, as well as your commitment to your organization and society, or do you stand by while others take the limelight, the credit and the success? It is an easy choice to make, but perhaps more difficult to commit to in the long term.

Once you start establishing a reputation as a leader with something to say, people will expect to hear from you, and on a regular basis. They will turn to you for ideas and advice and they will expect great things from you. They will come to rely on your wisdom and innovation, especially in challenging times. It is easy to see why some reluctant leaders stay in the shadows. But the best ideas are shared in a spirit of progress and love, always moving forward and not looking back, caring more about the people you help and less about yourself.

You know how to do it. But it is never about the *how* and always about the *why*. Do you have a strong enough reason to start (or continue) on this journey? The journey of the REAL thought leader is fast-paced and exciting, fascinating and full of adventure. If you decide to go boldly into the arena, you will not be disappointed. The riches that you seek are just within your grasp, and you must decide to reach out and grab them.

REAL Wealth

If you are willing to be REAL, you will become wealthy. I like to call it REAL wealth because you become rich in a way that benefits you, the people around you and society in general. As I said before, wealth means much more than how much money you have in your bank account. REAL wealth is a sense of fulfilment and well-being in any area of your life. If, at the end of your life, you were able to say that you fulfilled your potential, that you engaged with others and shared your most important ideas and views, and that you left a legacy for your peers, mentors and clients as well as your family and friends, then I think you would be deemed wealthier than someone who lived without sharing of himself in that way.

Where Can You Go for Help and to Find out More?

My study of REAL thought leaders will be an ongoing one. If you have thoughts and comments on this subject and would like to help me progress my thinking and create the kind of shifts in society that I know are possible, then please join me on my journey. Help me to encourage others to be more visible, more vocal and more valuable. Lead by example. Share your best ideas every day.

I will continue to look for and create tools and resources to help people discover, distil and distribute their wisdom in ways that improve as many lives as possible. Look out for future books, articles and other products on this important subject. You have a golden opportunity to share your wisdom with the world. Stay in touch and let me know what you're thinking. I will write about you if you give me some REAL messages and I will help you become the best REAL thought leader you can be. That is my mission and that is my promise.

About the Author

Mindy Gibbins-Klein is a specialist in turning experts into thought leaders and published authors and has helped hundred of business leaders around the world gain recognition as thought leaders and experts in their fields. She does this by showing them how to create the best possible books, ebooks and articles with which to raise their game and become more well known for what they do. As a Thought Leadership Executive Coach, Mindy regularly works with business leaders with her REAL Thought Leaders methodology, enabling them to raise their profile and deliver presentations and speeches with greater impact, and emphasis.

A native New Yorker, residing in the UK, Mindy owns and operates two successful businesses. She is founder & CEO of The Book Midwife® and CEO & owner of Ecademy Press: the cooperative publishing house for business authors.

Mindy has an MBA in International Business, is a trained coach and marketing consultant with over 18 years of experience in the corporate world, largely running marketing departments. She is a sought-after international motivational business speaker and is a regular media contributor.

Book Mindy to Speak

Mindy Gibbins-Klein is a dynamic and engaging speaker who turns business professionals into REAL thought leaders and students into entrepreneurial thinkers. She is available for keynote presentations and workshops on thought leadership, writing and publishing.

Mindy's most popular topics:

"How to Be a REAL Thought Leader"
"Turning Top Talent into Thought Leaders"
"Winning by Thinking - Creating a Culture of Thought Leadership in Your Organization"

Please visit www.mindygk.com or call +44 (0) 845 003 8848 for more information.

Mindy's companies:

 www.bookmidwife.com

 www.ecademy-press.com

Lightning Source UK Ltd.
Milton Keynes UK
UKOW020636051211

183217UK00001B/2/P